Contents

Introduction

THE ANXIETY EPIDEMIC is Volume 351 in the *ISSUES* series. The aim of the series is to offer current, diverse information about important issues in our world, from a UK perspective.

ABOUT THE ANXIETY EPIDEMIC

In recent years there has been a sharp rise in the number of young people seeking help because of anxiety. The constant pressure of social media and demands of schoolwork are just some of the contributing factors to this trend. This book explores different types of anxiety disorders, alongside triggers, symptoms and coping strategies.

OUR SOURCES

Titles in the *ISSUES* series are designed to function as educational resource books, providing a balanced overview of a specific subject.

The information in our books is comprised of facts, articles and opinions from many different sources, including:

◆   Newspaper reports and opinion pieces

◆   Website factsheets

◆   Magazine and journal articles

◆   Statistics and surveys

◆   Government reports

◆   Literature from special interest groups.

A NOTE ON CRITICAL EVALUATION

Because the information reprinted here is from a number of different sources, readers should bear in mind the origin of the text and whether the source is likely to have a particular bias when presenting information (or when conducting their research). It is hoped that, as you read about the many aspects of the issues explored in this book, you will critically evaluate the information presented.

It is important that you decide whether you are being presented with facts or opinions. Does the writer give a biased or unbiased report? If an opinion is being expressed, do you agree with the writer? Is there potential bias to the 'facts' or statistics behind an article?

ASSIGNMENTS

In the back of this book, you will find a selection of assignments designed to help you engage with the articles you have been reading and to explore your own opinions. Some tasks will take longer than others and there is a mixture of design, writing and research-based activities that you can complete alone or in a group.

FURTHER RESEARCH

At the end of each article we have listed its source and a website that you can visit if you would like to conduct your own research. Please remember to critically evaluate any sources that you consult and consider whether the information you are viewing is accurate and unbiased.

Useful Websites

www.anxietyuk.org.uk

www.befrienders.org

www.blurtitout.org

www.cam.ac.uk

www.goodtoknow.co.uk

www.headstogether.org.uk

www.healthline.com

www.independent.co.uk

www.inews.co.uk

www.kcl.ac.uk/cadat

www.medicalnewstoday.com

www.mentalhealth.org.uk

www.mind.org.uk

www.nopanic.org.uk

www.ons.gov.uk

www.open.edu

www.psychologytoday.com

www.rethink.org

www.samaritans.org

www.theconversation.com

www.theguardian.com

www.time-to-change.org.uk

www.timewith.co.uk

www.youngminds.org.uk

The Anxiety Epidemic

Editor: Tracy Biram

Volume 351

Independence Educational Publishers

First published by Independence Educational Publishers

The Studio, High Green

Great Shelford

Cambridge CB22 5EG

England

ISBN-13: 978 1 86168 807 1

Printed in Great Britain

Zenith Print Group

Chapter 1

About anxiety

What is anxiety?

Anxiety is a normal, if unpleasant, part of life, and it can affect us all in different ways and at different times. Whereas stress is something that will come and go as the external factor causing it (be it a work, relationship or money problem, etc.) comes and goes, anxiety is something that can persist whether or not the cause is clear to the sufferer.

Anxiety can make a person imagine that things in their life are worse than they really are, and prevent them from confronting their fears. Often they will think they are going mad, or that some psychological imbalance is at the heart of their woes. What is important is the recognition that anxiety is normal and exists due to a set of bodily functions that have existed in us from our cave-man days.

Back then, we were equipped with an internal alarm system designed to protect us from the dangers surrounding us in the wild. This system would make us hyper-alert by giving us a boost of adrenaline that would increase the heart rate and boost the amount of oxygen going to our limbs so we were better able to fight or run from danger. This is known as the 'fight or flight' response. The 'butterflies in the stomach' feeling that many associate with anxiety is this mechanism kicking in, but instead of being used to avoid immediate danger, it is often wrongly and inappropriately activated in a person during normal, everyday situations when stress has built up, often unknowingly.

Some people have a very identifiable cause for their anxiety; a traumatic incident, lots of stressors or have undergone a significant life event (moving house, getting divorced, having surgery). However, some people don't have an identifiable cause for their anxiety and it causes them some distress. One way of thinking about your anxiety is to imagine your stress levels as being like a bucket of water. If we keep adding stressors to the bucket (even tiny ones like the school run or commuting to work), over time it fills up until one day it overflows. This can be a good way of looking at anxiety as it explains why sometimes it can seem to come out of the blue with no significant trigger. However, what has happened is that the trigger was just a very small stressor that tipped us over the edge and allowed our bucket to overflow. What we need is a leaky bucket with lots of holes in to reduce your overall stress levels. Each one of these holes could be something positive that you do to manage your anxiety, such as yoga, exercise, reading, listening to music or spending time with friends or family.

Symptoms of anxiety

People often experience physical, psychological and behavioural symptoms when they feel anxious or stressed.

Some of the most common physical symptoms of anxiety are:

- Increased heart rate
- Increased muscle tension
- 'Jelly legs'
- Tingling in the hands and feet
- Hyperventilation (over-breathing)
- Dizziness
- Difficulty in breathing
- Wanting to use the toilet more often
- Feeling sick
- Tight band across the chest area
- Tension headaches
- Hot flushes
- Increased perspiration
- Dry mouth
- Shaking
- Choking sensations
- Palpitations.

Some of the most common psychological symptoms (the thoughts or altered perceptions we have) of anxiety are:

◆ Thinking that you may lose control and/or go 'mad'

◆ Thinking that you might die

◆ Thinking that you may have a heart attack/be sick/faint/have a brain tumour

◆ Feeling that people are looking at you and observing your anxiety

◆ Feeling as though things are speeding up/slowing down

◆ Feeling detached from your environment and the people in it

◆ Feeling like wanting to run away/escape from the situation

◆ Feeling on edge and alert to everything around you.

The most common behavioural symptom (the things we do when we are anxious) is avoidance. Although avoiding an anxiety-provoking situation produces immediate relief from the anxiety, it is only a short-term solution. This means that whilst it may seem like avoiding is the best thing to do at the time, the anxiety often returns the next time that you face the situation and avoiding it will only psychologically reinforce the message that there is danger.

The problem with avoidance is that you never get to find out whether your fear about the situation and what would happen is actually true.

September 2019

What causes anxiety?

No one knows exactly what causes anxiety problems, but there probably lots of factors involved. Here are some things which make anxiety problems more likely to happen.

Can anxiety problems be inherited genetically?

Research shows that having a close relative with anxiety problems increases your chances of experiencing anxiety problems yourself. But at the moment there is not enough evidence to show whether this is because we share some genetic factors that make us more vulnerable to developing anxiety, or because we learn particular ways of thinking and behaving from our parents and other family members as we grow up.

Past or childhood experiences

Difficult experiences in childhood, adolescence or adulthood are a common trigger for anxiety problems. Going through stress and trauma is likely to have a particularly big impact if it happens when you're very young. Experiences which can trigger anxiety problems include things like:

◆ physical or emotional abuse

◆ neglect

◆ losing a parent

◆ being bullied or being socially excluded.

Having parents who don't treat you warmly, are overprotective or are emotionally inconsistent can also be a factor.

Your current life situation

Current issues or problems in your life can also trigger anxiety. For example:

◆ exhaustion or a build up of stress

◆ long working hours

◆ being out of work

◆ feeling under pressure while studying or in work

◆ having money problems

◆ homelessness or housing problems

◆ losing someone close to you

◆ feeling lonely or isolated

◆ being bullied, harassed or abused.

Physical or mental health problems

Other health problems can sometimes cause anxiety, or might make it worse. For example:

◆ **Physical health problems** – living with a serious, ongoing or life-threatening physical health condition can sometimes trigger anxiety.

◆ **Other mental health problems** – it's also common to develop anxiety while living with other mental health problems, such as depression.

Drugs and medication

Anxiety can sometimes be a side effect of taking:

◆ some psychiatric medications

◆ some medications for physical health problems

◆ recreational drugs or alcohol.

Could diet be a factor?

Some types of food or drink can trigger symptoms of anxiety or panic, or make them worse. These include sugar and caffeine.

September 2017 – to be revised in 2020

Anxiety disorders

Anxiety disorders can affect work, home, social life and relationships. They can cause stress and worry not only to the sufferer but to the people around them too.

Obsessive compulsive disorder (OCD)

OCD can vary in severity from very mild to severe and can take many different forms. Some people are bothered by upsetting thoughts that they cannot get rid of no matter how hard they try; other people may find they feel compelled to wash or check things, even though logically they know there is no need. When people are troubled by their obsessional problems they can experience very high levels of anxiety and distress, it can take up lots of time and interfere with almost every aspect of their life.

Hoarding disorder

Treatment for Hoarding Disorder is provided to help people who are living in cluttered homes. People collect large amounts of possessions for many different reasons (for example, items may be kept as they will 'come in handy some day' or because they appear beautiful, or that they must be recycled or reused) and it is very difficult for people to actually use or part with these items. Often people in cluttered homes are also suffering from other anxiety problems or depression and they can suffer from poor physical health too. CADAT has links with the local boroughs and work closely with housing departments to ensure that people with hoarding problems are treated sensitively when access to their homes is required (for gas checks, etc.)

Body dysmorphic disorder (BDD)

Body Dysmorphic Disorder (BDD) is a body image problem. It is defined as a preoccupation with one or more perceived defects in one's appearance which other people may hardly notice or may not believe to be important. In addition, the symptoms must also either cause significant distress or handicap. For example, someone with BDD might avoid certain social and public situations to prevent themselves from feeling uncomfortable and worrying that people are rating them negatively. Alternatively, a person may enter

such situations but remain very self conscious. He or she may camouflage themselves excessively to hide their perceived defect by using heavy make-up, brushing their hair in a particular way, changing their posture, or wearing heavy clothes. They may spend several hours a day thinking about their perceived defect and asking themselves questions that cannot be answered (for example, 'Why was I born this way?', 'If only my nose was straighter and smaller') They may feel compelled to repeat certain time-consuming behaviours including:

(i) Checking their appearance in a mirror or reflective surface;

(ii) Seeking reassurance about their appearance;

(iii) Checking by feeling their skin with their fingers;

(iv) Cutting or combing their hair to make it 'just so';

(v) Picking their skin to make it smooth

(vi) Comparing themselves against models in magazines or people in the street.

Post-traumatic stress disorder (PTSD)

PTSD develops following exposure to one or more traumatic events. These events cause intense fear during which the individual may feel like they (or someone very close to them) are about to die or experience serious harm. Traumatic events go beyond daily stressful events and can include: physical and sexual assault; accidents and road traffic accidents; natural disasters; witnessing someone being badly injured or killed; experiencing war and torture.

People experience a combination of the following symptoms:

(i) Re-experiencing symptoms including: Unwanted thoughts and memories of the trauma, flashbacks, and nightmares;

(ii) Avoidance symptoms such as avoiding talking about the trauma, thinking about it or feelings associated with it, and avoiding reminders of the trauma such as people, places or activities;

(iii) Hyperarousal symptoms such as being overly alert or watchful and feeling jumpy.

Social anxiety disorder (SAD)

SAD is an anxiety disorder in which people experience a distressing amount of anxiety whenever they are in a feared social or performance situation. A social situation is any situation that involves interacting with other people. A performance situation is a situation in which a person is concerned that what they are doing in public is being scrutinised or judged by others. Although it is normal for

(vii) chest pain or discomfort;

(viii) numbness or tingling sensations;

(ix) feeling as if you or your surroundings are unreal;

(x) nausea or churning stomach;

(xi) choking;

(xii) fear of dying;

(xiii) fear of losing control or going crazy.

Panic disorder with agoraphobia is anxiety about being in places or situations for fear of having a panic attack or panicky feelings. Situations may include being away from home, queuing, travelling on public transport or using lifts. Some people avoid these situations completely. Others force themselves into feared situations, but feel anxious and panicky throughout.

people to sometimes feel anxious in social situations, SAD is diagnosed when the social anxiety significantly interferes in a person's life and stops them from doing things that they would otherwise like to do.

People with SAD are concerned that they will do or say something that will be humiliating or embarrassing. They often fear that other people will see them blush, sweat, tremble or otherwise look anxious.

Panic disorder (PD) and panic disorder with agoraphobia

People with Panic Disorder have had recurrent unexpected panic attacks, are often very apprehensive about having more attacks, and may change their behaviour or lifestyle as a result of these. Panic attacks usually come on very suddenly and reach their peak within ten minutes. The peak generally lasts for five to ten minutes, but it can take much longer for all the anxiety to subside. In a panic, normal fear reactions are happening at the wrong time and the body's 'alarm system', which is designed to help you deal with emergencies, gets triggered off, exactly as if you were in real danger. People are often afraid that they may collapse, lose consciousness, have a heart attack, lose control, go mad or even die. This intense fear is normally accompanied by four or more symptoms from the following:

(i) palpitations or rapid heart rate;

(ii) breathlessness;

(iii) feeling unsteady, dizzy, light-headed or faint;

(iv) trembling or shaking;

(v) sweating;

(vi) having a hot flush or chills;

Specific phobia disorders (e.g. spiders, driving, flying, etc.) (SP)

Specific phobia is an anxiety disorder in which there is a marked fear or avoidance of a specific object or situation. Common examples of specific phobias include:

(i) The sight of blood or injury;

(ii) Birds;

(iii) Insects;

(iv) Animals;

(v) Heights;

(vi) Dentists;

(vii) Spiders.

The fear revolves around becoming anxious when in contact with the object or situation and immediately provokes an anxiety response or acute symptoms of panic. At this stage the person may wish to escape or avoid any contact with the object, situation or fear. On occasions life activities can become restricted because of it. The person is able to recognise the fear is exaggerated but is unable to eliminate the fear or reduce the avoidance.

Specific phobia of vomit (SPOV or emetophobia)

Emetophobia is the common name for a Specific Phobia of Vomiting (SPOV). This is an anxiety disorder in which an individual has an overwhelming fear of vomiting whilst

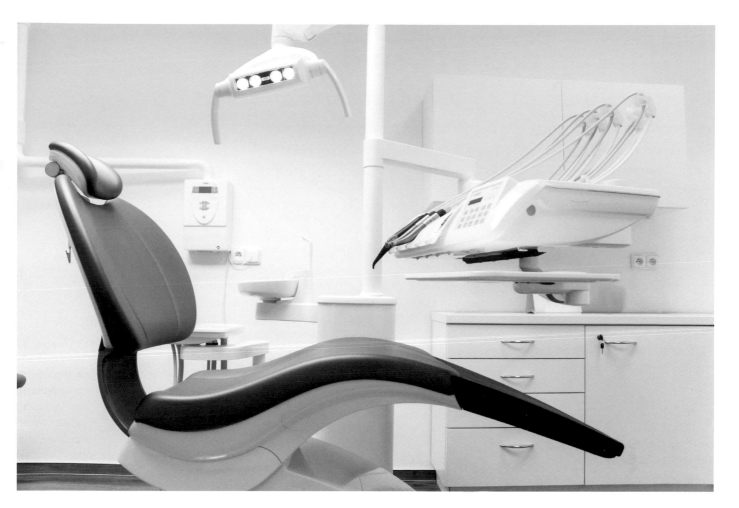

alone or in public. They may also have a fear of witnessing others vomiting.

Sufferers can experience a combination of the following:

(i) Complete preoccupation with this fear;

(ii) Panic;

(iii) Fear of losing control;

(iv) Fear of becoming very ill;

(v) Fear that others will find them repulsive.

As a result, people try too hard to avoid a wide range of situations or activities that they believe might increase the risk of vomiting. This can significantly interfere in a person's life and stop them from doing things that they would otherwise like to do.

General anxiety disorder (GAD)

We all worry from time to time, as if silently talking to ourselves about possible bad outcomes. Uncontrollable worry is common at times of stress, and is the central feature of Generalised Anxiety Disorder (GAD), which is a common, chronic and disabling problem. Uncontrollable worry may be due to:

(i) unhelpful mental habits which focus on threat,

(ii) difficulty deliberately shifting mental focus away from threat.

Health anxiety (HA)

Health anxiety is characterised by preoccupation with a fear of developing a serious illness, or with the belief that one already has an undiagnosed serious illness. The preoccupation persists despite medical reassurance. Sufferers can misinterpret normal physical sensations, such as dizziness or tiredness, as evidence of a severe illness. Common examples include:

(i) A headache may be misinterpreted as a brain tumour;

(ii) A lump in one's body may be misinterpreted as cancer;

(iii) Feelings of unreality may be misinterpreted as a sign of schizophrenia. Medical information from doctors, other people, the media and from the internet is also often misinterpreted.

This marked fear may cause people to try to avoid and/or distract themselves from their thoughts and feelings or to escape from or avoid situations that remind them of illness or death, e.g. avoiding going to the doctor or reading about illness in the media. Alternatively people may seek repeated reassurance from friends, doctors or repeated visits to A&E departments to find out the cause of their symptoms. This preoccupation with health can also significantly affect relationships with family and friends as the sufferer may

Is there an anxiety epidemic?

Are we still plagued by the same forms of anxiety as our ancient ancestors?

By Graham C. L. Davey Ph.D., Professor of Psychology, University of Sussex, author of The Anxiety Epidemic: The Causes of our Modern Day Anxieties

The way that anxiety manifests itself has not really changed over the centuries and we're still plagued by the same forms of anxiety disorder as our ancient ancestors, but the things that trigger our anxiety have certainly changed. We still experience many traditional causes of anxiety such as poor health, difficult relationships, unemployment, poverty and disadvantage, loneliness, work stress, and exposure to violence, trauma and conflict. Even in our modern world, some of these traditional sources of anxiety are on the increase. These include loneliness; relationship factors such as divorce; violence and abuse – including childhood abuse and neglect; increased working hours and more stressful work procedures; and a general sense of lack of control over our own destinies – especially amongst our youngsters who are introduced to the possibility of failure earlier and earlier in their lives as a result of increased systematic educational testing. Thankfully, some of the traditional causes of anxiety are generally on the decline, factors such as poverty, poor health and to some extent unemployment. But they leave in their place some new anxieties, such as income inequality, living with long-term disability, and the stresses of modern-day job seeking.

In addition, modern technology has provided some entirely new sources of anxiety for the present generations. These include 24-hour perpetual connectivity, the need to multitask across a range of different activities, and regular increasingly emotive news alerts and doomsday scenarios. Very soon almost every appliance in our houses will be connected to the Internet, fuelling fears of identity theft, data hacking, phishing, grooming and trolling. Even that bastion of modern-day living, the computer, brings with it daily worrisome hassles that include crashing hard drives, forgotten passwords, and the frustration of daily transactions that begin to seem strangely distant when all we'd like to do is speak to a real person. Riding on the back of our daily computer stresses is the perpetual connectivity provided by social media. The first recognisable social media sites were created in the mid-1990s, so most youngsters under the age of 20 will never have lived without the curse of social media. And a curse it can be. Social media use is closely associated with social anxiety and loneliness and can generate feelings of disconnectedness when we view what seems like the rich lives and social successes of others. A consequence of social media use is that youngsters count their social success in terms of metrics such as the number of friends they have on sites like Facebook, not the number of genuine confidants they have – confidants who would be true friends in times of difficulty and need.

To supplement this rash of new, modern anxieties is a gradual shift in the social ethos surrounding anxiety. This change has been almost contradictory in the messages it sends to us. We're told anxiety is a legitimate response to the stresses of modern living, and anxiety is almost considered a status symbol that signals how busy and successful you are. But we're increasingly told that anxiety is an emotion in need of treatment. Diagnostic categories for anxiety problems have burgeoned over the past 30 years, the pharmaceutical industry is keener than ever to medicalise anxiety and sell us a pharmaceutical solution for it, and increasing numbers of social campaigns increase awareness of mental health problems such as anxiety, valiantly attempt to destigmatise it, and then help us to identify it and seek treatment for it.

But it would be irresponsible of me to claim that all is doom and gloom on the anxiety epidemic front. Roughly one in five people regularly suffer distressingly high levels of anxiety but there's no significant evidence that this ratio has increased over the years. But even if that ratio stays the same, as populations grow, more and more people will suffer anxiety and will be seeking treatment for it as awareness of mental health problems increases. On the other side of the coin, two out of five people tend to experience only low levels of anxiety, and will rarely need to seek treatment unless they encounter extreme life events that elicit extreme responses.

New psychosocial treatments for anxiety are continually being developed, and we now have specialised CBT (cognitive behavioural therapy) programmes for most if not all of the main anxiety disorders. In addition, access to basic forms of CBT for common mental health problems such as anxiety has increased significantly in a number of countries with the successful introduction of programmes such as IAPS (Improving Access to Psychological Therapies), and computer-based CBT for anxiety is an increasingly effective medium through which sufferers can be helped to recover. But even with the most successful evidence-based psychotherapy and pharmaceutical procedures, we're still some way from helping 100% of people to recover from anxiety disorders, and some anxiety disorders such as OCD and GAD can be debilitating life-long conditions resistant to both current medications and psychotherapies. To improve the range of interventions available we need significantly more funding for mental health research. The level of funding for mental health research is pitiful when compared with that provided for research into other medical problems, and arguably much of the funding that is available goes to medical and neuroscience programmes rather than the psychological research that would be needed to develop more effective, evidence-based talking therapies.

So, is there an anxiety epidemic? Contemporary definitions of the term 'epidemic' no longer allude to disease as a necessary condition, and consider an epidemic anything that negatively impacts on the health or welfare of a large number of people in a population. One in five people in the UK suffer high levels of anxiety at any one time; one in nine people worldwide will experience an anxiety disorder in any one year; anxiety prevents you from working, learning, or performing your social and family responsibilities to your full potential; anxiety and stress account for over a third of all work-related ill health and costs over £100 billion in England each year in lost productivity and reduced quality of life; and anxiety can kill – even sub-clinical levels of anxiety can increase the risk of mortality by 20%. So, yes, we do have a modern anxiety epidemic, but then so have most previous generations. The difference is that in our modern era we have a whole set of new and evolving anxieties and a growing awareness of anxiety as a potentially distressing and disabling state. We'll need to rise to the contemporary challenges that this presents in terms of understanding the causes of anxiety and the suffering it conveys, dealing with the economic cost to society that anxiety imposes, developing new and more effective evidence-based intervention and prevention programmes, and providing more realistic levels of funding for mental health services and research.

6 November 2019

Feel better now? The rise and rise of the anxiety economy

By Eva Wiseman

Consider the squishy. The point of the squishy, a palm-sized mass of polyurethane in the shape of a fruit or a croissant or a unicorn cat, occasionally scented with strawberry, is to squish. The point of the squishy is to be held in the hand of a person with energy that needs redirecting and for them to direct it into the soft heart of the squishy, to squeeze it into almost nothing in their palm, only for it to reinflate again, asking for more. In 1988 a TV writer called Alex Carswell threw a pen at a photo of his mother after a stressful phone call with his boss. It gave him an idea.

It was the 'Age of Stress' – the *Daily Mirror* (among other newspapers) had identified it as 'a killer' – and so the perfect time for Carswell to launch his 'stress ball'. By the 1990s it had evolved from something squishy designed to be thrown into something squishy designed to be squeezed, and to be squeezed mainly by kids, who collected them in small scented families in their rucksacks. In a 2015 study of patients undergoing varicose vein surgery, those that handled stress balls reported feeling 'less anxious'.

'When you're stressed, your body tightens up,' says Dr Kathleen Hall, founder of the Stress Institute, explaining why throwing or squeezing something feels good, 'so a physical release helps to let go of some of that energy.' Carswell was not the first person to link a calming of the mind to a busy-ness of a hand – in 206 BC, the Han dynasty in China trained to stay mentally focused during combat by squeezing walnuts. The croissant squishy comes from an ancient place.

That repeated action led to fidget spinners becoming one of the most popular items bought on Amazon in 2017. They were not simply triangles of plastic; they were a stress-relief toy, a treatment for ADHD, an answer to smartphone addiction, a modern rosary – and the cause of moral panic, as teachers confiscated them as contraband. They were the stars of a growing anxiety economy.

Alongside products designed purely as medical aids, such as meditation apps, there is a thriving offshoot of lifestyle goods marketed through their anxiety-relieving qualities.

Product innovation oriented around anxiety (encompassing stress, mood and sleep) spans nearly 30 different categories, including chocolate, yogurt, air fresheners, fabric conditioners and skincare. There is a company called Body Vibes which, for £30, will sell you a pack of anti-anxiety stickers that 'rebalance the energy frequency in our bodies'. Throw a squishy ball in the high street and you're likely to hit something to cure your stress.

If the 80s were the age of stress, this is the age of anxiety, with 30% of Britons experiencing an anxiety disorder during their lifetime. 'The NHS Adult Psychiatric Morbidity Survey, published in 2016, indicated that anxiety and depression affected about one in six people,' confirms consultant clinical psychologist Dr Nihara Krause, founder of youth mental health charity Stem4. This rise in anxiety coincides with a crisis in mental health care. And long waits for treatment often lead to more complications, and the problems multiply, a kind of silent mitosis, leading to even more pressure on the NHS as well as the patient. This has created a market for domestic anxiety cures that can be bought online, and fast.

'Because community services are cut,' says Krause, 'there is little in the way of help for those who are unwell but don't meet the threshold for acceptance to established services.

'And those who are severe can't access help because specialist services are underresourced. I am really keen on providing early intervention tools that are evidence-based and are therefore effective. Sadly there are a lot of products on the market that are not tested for their efficacy.'

Developed in the early 1990s by American engineer Catherine Hettinger, fidget spinners were designed as a calming tool, but when they went mainstream, marketers built on their medical promise simply by adjusting the aesthetics – much like adult colouring books, the publishing phenomenon of 2015 which sold millions due to their therapeutic mental health benefits; and more recently, the weighted blanket. In 2017 the sleep-health industry was worth between $30 billion and $40 billion. Mattresses were being marketed like iPads, iPads were swollen with sleep apps and the weighted blanket, a therapeutic aid, was redesigned as a chic lifestyle accessory.

A fleece Gravity Blanket costs £149 and is the colour of a Manchester sky. 'Studies have shown that using a weighted blanket increases the level of serotonin and melatonin as well as reduces cortisol,' says its website. The company was founded by psychologist Joanna Goliszek. She ran a therapy centre in Poland, working with, she tells me, 'an autistic boy with an urgent need for a weighted blanket. But most products available on the market were simply not affordable.' She started to manufacture them in her apartment and, in 2017, launched across Europe, reshifting their focus, the new customer being 'everyone'. On Instagram, there are almost 32,000 posts with the #weightedblanket hashtag, including one from Tori Spelling, naked but for her blanket, explaining how it has changed her life by helping her sleep. Despite the fact that companies had been manufacturing them primarily for children with autism-spectrum disorders for many years (leading, as they went mainstream, to claims of appropriation), Time magazine named 'blankets that ease anxiety' one of the best inventions of 2018, quoting figures from a sleek US start-up (also called Gravity, no relation) which had already sold $18 million worth of blankets.

In early 2018, in her New Yorker essay 'The Seductive Confinement of a Weighted Blanket in an Anxious Time', Jia Tolentino wrote that their success "arrived deep into a period when many Americans were beginning their emails with reflexive, panicked condolences about the news". It was no coincidence that they had become a million-dollar business when much of the world felt like it needed to be put to bed. They had co-opted a familiar coping strategy (the feeling of being held) by repackaging a product that originated to assist a vulnerable community and selling it to people who felt anxious, i.e. almost everyone.

Mine arrived in a large box and, when I opened it, the blanket felt extremely cold. It took some effort to unfold it and then transport it to my bed – carrying the blanket felt not like carrying something objectively heavy like bricks or bags of tins, but like carrying a very light thing when you're coming down with flu. I arranged myself under its grey soft weight, and then I fell asleep.

In the morning I woke in the same position. Unlike other anxiety aids, which encourage movement, fiddling, this large flat beanbag prevents movement. You are gently forced into a comforting stillness. Brushing my teeth the morning after a deep, deep sleep, I swilled the phrase 'self-care' around my mouth.

In its earliest iteration it was used by doctors advising elderly patients on how to stay healthy at home, but by the late 1960s people used it more often in reference to the doctors themselves, having recognised that those in emotionally wearing professions could only look after others if they first looked after themselves. With the rise of the civil rights movement, self-care became political. Women and people of colour insisted that an autonomy over one's body was necessary to fight racist and sexist systems, and indeed to survive. The phrase has since spread and mutated to include such diverse applications as gardening, antidepressants and peeling foot masks.

Today one of the places the phrase is most visible is in online articles about skincare routines, the ritual massaging in of oils and perfecting lotions, where the user is encouraged to concentrate less on how their skin looks tomorrow, but more on the mindful motions of looking after themselves.

'I know now that anxiety doesn't really ever go away entirely,' wrote Olivia Muenter in an article called 'How My Beauty Routine Helps With My Anxiety', for Bustle, 'but sometimes it shuts the hell up. And, for me, it's often the quietest during my beauty routine.' She describes the action of moisturising as if it was meditation. Her skincare routine 'pushes [her worries] away and what I'm left with is the simple act of doing something that makes me feel good'.

It's at skincare that two arms of the anxiety economy cross, with the rise of CBD (Cannabidiol) beauty. Owing to the increased interest in cannabis for medicinal use, the CBD (a non-psychoactive chemical compound found in marijuana) industry is expected to reach an estimated value of $22 billion by 2022, with products including (but not limited to) teas, ice cream, vapes and hair conditioner. Last year Estée Lauder became one of the first mainstream beauty brands to release cannabis-infused products, alongside a growing list of smaller companies that included it in their brightening face creams, soaps, moisturising oils and mascaras, with the promise that CBD has anti-inflammatory properties. Though some claim it to be "stressrelieving", simply by containing CBD their anxiety-relieving side effects are implicit.

A cynic might point out that considering the pressure the cosmetic industry has maintained in pushing customers to achieve unrealistic beauty standards, their new insistence that their primary role is to reduce anxiety is ironic. Evidence of CBD's efficacy in skincare is largely anecdotal and a study in the *Journal of the American Medical Association* found widespread mislabelling of CBD products sold online. There is a similar issue in all areas of the CBD industry – complications around legalisation have made it hard for researchers to discover what it actually does. Small trials suggest that CBD could be effective in treating anxiety, but only in far larger doses than are usually offered. While a product can boast in its marketing materials that CBD reduces anxiety, there's no proof that the product itself – whether oil or tea – does anything at all.

It's something that bothers Dr Krause. Having seen how the NHS has had to 'unofficially perform triage when it comes to crisis-level mental health conditions' – meaning that people with anxiety disorders are often pushed to the back of the queue – she's aware of the brands profiting from this. 'The market seems saturated. There are a number of companies that are trading on fake news to promote a whole range of products that are meant to help with mental health problems but without any evidence base to them. Given that we are dealing with a vulnerable population it is questionable how ethical producing these tools without evidence base and systematic review of efficacy is.'

The anxiety economy shows no signs of shrinking, with white noise machines, salt lamps and meditation headbands advertised alongside yoga selfies on Instagram. Aids for anxiety disorders in 2019 are branded like covetable scented candles – scrolling through the products, one starts to think of it as a small but universal ill like dry lips or shaving rash, and one just as easily treated. Which, it could be argued, threatens to normalise this mental illness; to recode it as a standard part of modern life, rather than something that requires medical attention. If one in six adults suffer from depression and anxiety disorders, that means there are five who have no need to be part of this niche market, and yet still, under the blanket-style weight of advertising, find their thumbs hovering over the button.

Is anxiety itself being commodified? This is a disorder that can stoke its own fire – worrying about anxiety can make it worse. Could it be that these products, rather than simply easing anxiety, are in fact propagating it, meaning healthy people self-diagnose an illness they don't understand? And what about the causes? Is a £30 'anti-anxiety sticker' really just a plaster for a larger wound?

Psychoanalyst Michael Currie notes that we rarely deal with the causes of anxiety – job insecurity for example, or social isolation – when trying to treat it. Writing in *The Monthly*, he says: 'Anxiety-as-disease is treated much like an infection, as if the symptoms were a bacterium that should be eradicated.' Buying a blanket is significantly easier than changing the world.

Closing down my emails to Dr Krause, I realise I've been absentmindedly squeezing the scared-cat squishy that sits on my desk. Does it work? Debatable. Does it matter? Also debatable. Ten years ago, a study was conducted with sufferers of social anxiety disorder.

Sufferers were asked to take part in a stressful public speaking event, before being treated for eight weeks and then doing it again. Assessed by psychiatrists, 40% of the patients showed an improvement in their symptoms, despite all having been given placebos. The act of using a product that says it will make us feel better may actually make us feel better; for mild anxiety, the cure may not be in the squishy, but in the mind. Slowly, in my palm, the cat expands.

Stress busters

Anxiety has become a multi-million pound industry – but here are some ways to combat it for free

Take regular exercise Aerobic exercises, such as jogging, swimming and cycling, encourage your brain to release serotonin, which can improve your mood. It also helps combat stress and release tension. Aim for at least two and a half hours a week.

Ditch the coffee It speeds up your heart rate and disrupts your sleep. If you're tired, it's harder to control anxious thoughts.

Contact support groups Go to anxietyuk.org.uk and mental health charity mind.org.uk – their services include talking therapies, crisis helplines, drop-in centres, training schemes, counselling and befriending.

Download a free app Catch It is a joint project launched by the universities of Liverpool and Manchester to help users better understand their moods; Elefriends is an online community from Mind and Verywellmind is an NHS mental health and well-being app designed to help with stress, anxiety and depression.

10 March 2019

Personal and economic well-being in the UK: April 2019 Office for National Statistics bulletin

While average anxiety levels reached a three-year low in 2018, about 10.3 million people continued to report high anxiety scores.

By Gueorguie Vassilev, Silvia Manclossi, Sunny Sidhu, Jack Yull and Ed Pyle from the Economic Well-being and Quality of Life Teams, Office for National Statistics

While average anxiety levels reached a three-year low in 2018, about 10.3 million people continued to report high anxiety scores. In the year ending December 2018, the average rating of anxiety in the UK reached its lowest level since the year ending December 2015. UK, average ratings of anxiety for the year ending December 2012 to December 2018.

Alongside increases in real household disposable income, there has been an improvement in the average ratings of anxiety. Between the years ending December 2017 and December 2018, anxiety scores fell across the UK from 2.91 to 2.85 measured on a scale from 0 to 10. This was the lowest average rating of anxiety since the year ending

December 2015 and represents a decrease of 2.1% in the average anxiety across the UK. This was replicated in the average anxiety ratings across England, also showing similar improvements in reported levels of anxiety.

However, this is the only measure of personal well-being to show any significant change during this period. For the other measures of personal well-being – life satisfaction, feeling that the things done in life are worthwhile, and happiness – average ratings remained level with no significant changes since the year ending December 2016.

In addition to looking at average ratings, we also monitor potential inequalities in personal well-being by comparing

In the year ending December 2018, the average rating of anxiety in the UK reached its lowest level since the year ending December 2015

UK, average ratings of anxiety for the year ending December 2012 to December 2018

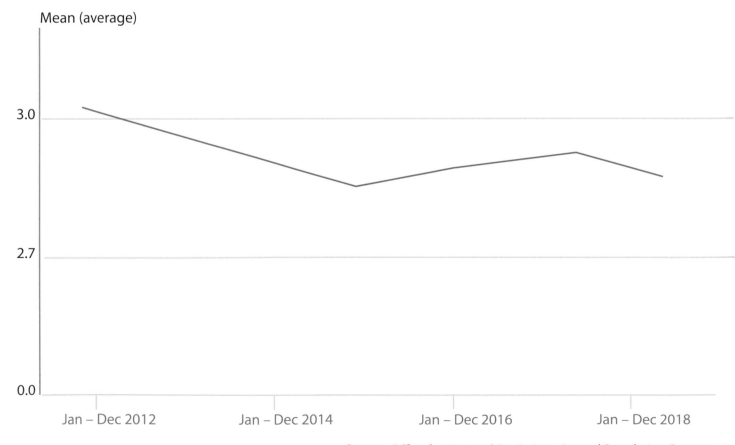

Source: Office for National Statistics – Annual Population Survey

About 10.3 million people continue to report 'high' levels of anxiety for the year ending December 2018

UK, yearly percentage change of 'very low' and 'high' levels of anxiety since year ending December 2012.

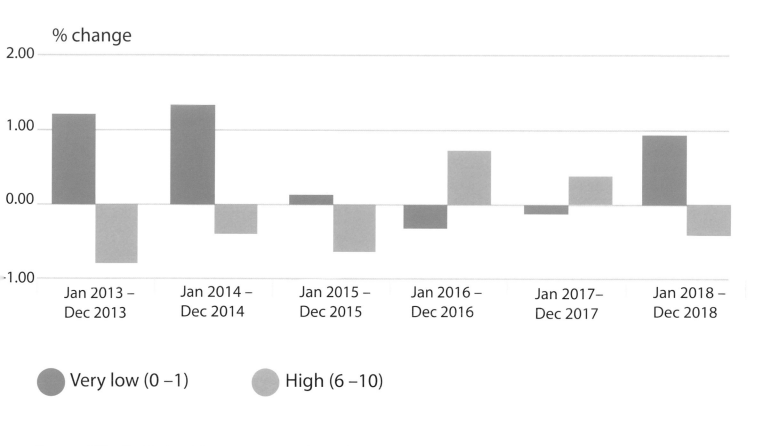

% change

Very low (0 –1)   High (6 –10)

Source: Office for National Statistics – Annual Population Survey

Notes:

'Very low' anxiety refers to those providing a rating of 0 to 1, 'high' anxiety refers to those reporting a score of 6 to 10 (on an 11-point scale from 0 to 10).

those rating each aspect of their well-being either at a very high level or a very low level.

During the years ending December 2017 and 2018, there was an increase in the people reporting very low levels of anxiety in the UK, from 40.2% to 41.2% of the population. This improvement in anxiety was driven by an increase in the very low ratings in England, rising from 39.9% to 41.1%. This change in the proportion of respondents reporting very low levels of anxiety is the biggest improvement since the year ending December 2014. However, in the year ending December 2018, among the UK population 19.7% or about 10.3 million people reported high levels of anxiety. There was no significant change compared with the year ending December 2017 (20.1%). The proportion of respondents reporting 'high' levels of anxiety has not seen an improvement since the year ending December 2013.

11 April 2019

How do anxiety and depression affect physical health?

By Ana Sandolu

Depression and anxiety may be just as bad for your health as smoking and obesity. However, cancer does not correlate with these mental health conditions. These are the main takeaways of a new study that investigates the physical health risks of these psychiatric conditions.

In the 17th century, Enlightenment philosopher Rene Descartes posited that the mind and the body were separate entities.

While this dualist idea has shaped much of modern science and thought, recent scientific advances show that the dichotomy between the mind and the body is a false one.

For instance, neuroscientist Antonio Damasio famously wrote the book he entitled *Descartes' error*' to prove precisely the point that our brains, emotions and judgment are much more intertwined than people previously believed.

The findings of a new study may further contribute to this latter argument. Aoife O'Donovan, Ph.D., of the Department of Psychiatry at the University of California San Francisco, and her colleague Andrea Niles, Ph.D., set out to examine the effects that psychiatric conditions, such as depression and anxiety, may have on a person's physical health.

The researchers investigated the health of more than 15,000 seniors over four years and published their findings in *Health Psychology*, the journal of the American Psychological Association.

Anxiety and depression similar to smoking

The study looked at the health data of 15,418 retirees who were 68 years old, on average. The data came from a governmental study that used interviews to assess the participants' symptoms of anxiety and depression.

The participants also answered questions about their weight, smoking status and medical conditions they had a diagnosis of. In addition, they provided information about weight recordings from hospital visits.

Of the total number of participants, O'Donovan and colleagues found that 16% had high levels of anxiety and depression, 31% had obesity, and 14% were smokers.

Those living with high levels of anxiety and depression were 65% more likely to develop a heart condition, 64% more likely to have a stroke, 50% more likely to develop high blood pressure and 87% percent more likely to have arthritis than people who did not have anxiety or depression.

'These increased odds are similar to those of participants who are smokers or are obese,' says O'Donovan. 'However,' she adds, 'for arthritis, high anxiety and depression seem to confer higher risks than smoking and obesity.'

Cancer not related to anxiety and stress

Of all the conditions investigated, the scientists found that cancer was the only one that did not correlate with anxiety and depression. These findings confirm previous studies, explain the researchers, but they run against the belief that many patients share.

'Our findings are in line with a lot of other studies showing that psychological distress is not a strong predictor of many types of cancer,' says O'Donovan.

'On top of highlighting that mental health matters for a whole host of medical illnesses, it is important that we promote these null findings. We need to stop attributing cancer diagnoses to histories of stress, depression and anxiety.'

– Aoife O'Donovan

'Anxiety and depression symptoms are strongly linked to poor physical health, yet these conditions continue to receive limited attention in primary care settings, compared to smoking and obesity,' Niles says.

O'Donovan adds that the findings highlight the 'long-term costs of untreated depression and anxiety [...] and serve as a reminder that treating mental health conditions can save money for health systems.'

'To our knowledge, this is the first study that directly compared anxiety and depression to obesity and smoking as prospective risk factors for disease onset in long-term studies,' says Niles.

In the United States, over 16 million people have had at least one episode of major depression in their lives. Also, again according to the National Institute of Mental Health, over 19% of adults in the US have had an anxiety disorder in the past year.

18 December 2018

Brexit anxiety shouldn't be over-medicalised – it is fuelling real political engagement

THE CONVERSATION

An article from **The Conversation.**

By Dan Degerman, Ph.D. Candidate in Philosphy, Lancaster University

With no deal in sight, people are justifiably anxious about Brexit. A new poll by the research company Britain Thinks found just under two-thirds of people surveyed believe the uncertainty over Brexit is bad for people's mental health.

Mental health experts are warning that these anxieties are indeed cause for concern. But their warnings may have serious political consequences.

Declaring Brexit-related anxiety a national phenomenon, BBC Radio 4's PM programme discussed this issue on March 28 – the day before the UK was scheduled to leave the EU. Listener accounts of Brexit anxiety were paired with expert 'remedies' for coping with the 'condition'. Among the experts was a GP, who urged that the best way to deal with Brexit anxiety was for people to take control of the things they can control, such as sleeping, eating, exercising and limiting their exposure to social media.

This might seem like reasonable advice. For some vulnerable people, it probably is. Anxiety is painful and can be debilitating. Yet there is something deeply suspect about framing the anxiety that people in general have about Brexit as an individual issue subject to medical expertise. First, Brexit anxiety clearly has a political cause. Second, framing it as a medical problem seemingly rests on the assumption that people are unable to influence the political

situation and that they should simply accept this and focus on themselves.

My research shows that the BBC's treatment of Brexit anxiety is far from an isolated example. Since the referendum on Britain's membership in the EU in June 2016, journalists, mental health experts and other observers have warned of the dire effects of Brexit anxiety. These warnings were particularly common and alarmist in the weeks and months following the referendum. Newspapers reported, with little evidence, that emotional people were flooding mental health clinics, which were creaking under the pressure. Therapists and psychiatrists reached out to offer their advice on how to deal with Brexit anxiety.

These experts called on anxious people to acknowledge their lack of control in the face of Brexit, disconnect from news and social media, and focus on the things that really matter, such as family, friends and work. Failure to follow this advice could mean spiralling into serious mental disorder. Some workplaces have taken this seriously, offering mental health resources and workshops to help their employees deal with their Brexit anxiety.

With anxiety comes action

Negative emotions have a bad reputation, especially in politics. Anxiety, anger and other emotions sometimes lead us to act rashly or without evidence. Still, I think most people recognise that negative emotions can also play a constructive political role. After all, we usually take political action because some perceived problem in the world has evoked negative emotions in us and we persist in our action partly because such emotions fuel us. By acting politically, we may not only address the cause of our distress, but, in the process, the joy of action may, at least for a time, replace our anxiety.

But emotions can only play this role if we are able to channel them into political issues, such as Brexit. The media portrayal of Brexit anxiety undermines this ability. It implies that the negative emotions people feel about Brexit are potential mental health problems to be solved by a personal change, even though these emotions evidently have political causes and solutions.

Worryingly, the Brexit anxiety narrative also incorporates the disempowering misconception that because ordinary people cannot control politics they might as well focus on other things. But if the past few years have shown us anything it's that not even the prime minister, Theresa May, can control political events. To paraphrase the political theorist Hannah Arendt: in politics, where we are always dealing with a plurality of ever-changing relationships between people, sovereign control is an illusion.

While the actions of ordinary people are obviously less powerful than those of elected politicians or business leaders, this doesn't mean that they are incapable of shaping political issues under the right conditions. Recent weeks have shown us some of what is possible when people are able to channel their emotions politically. The mass of people who marched on London in late March demanding a second referendum may not have stopped Brexit. Neither did the thousands of Brexit supporters who gathered outside parliament force it through. Yet their actions have already shaped political discourse and will continue to shape it in ways that we cannot anticipate. Expert warnings about the health risks of Brexit anxiety won't stop protests like this from happening. But, by perpetuating the idea that good, healthy citizens keep calm and leave politics to the politicians, they may well keep many people at home at a time when their involvement could determine the future of the country.

3 April 2019

Stress and anxiety in the digital age: The dark side of technology

What is it about new technology that is making many of us anxious and stressed? Dr Gini Harrison and Dr Mathijs Lucassen explore the top five stressors.

Technology is everywhere, and mobile phones have become an essential part of everyday life. According to Ofcom's 2017 figures, 94% of adults in the UK own a mobile phone; and over three-quarters of those are smartphones. And while mobile phones were originally designed to facilitate phone calls on the go, Deloitte's mobile consumer survey (2016) suggests a third of smartphone users don't actually make traditional voice calls at all. Instead, our phones are used as mobile computers, for checking email, shopping online, accessing news, downloading music and videos, engaging in social media, ordering food, looking at maps... the list goes on. We literally have the internet in our pocket at all times and can seemingly find out the answer to almost any question at the touch of a button. But while these advancements in technological functionality and access are amazing' they come at a cost.

There is evidence that we are becoming over-dependent, or even possibly addicted, to our phones. Think about how you feel when you realise you have forgotten your phone, or left it behind somewhere. It can be uncomfortable, can't it? In fact, recent research has shown that some people experience significant stress and anxiety when they are separated from their phones and can even exhibit withdrawal-like symptoms, comparable to those usually seen when someone has an addiction. Some research has even shown that high levels of engagement with smartphones and multimedia technology may be physically changing our brain structure and function.

So, what is it about technology that is making many of us anxious and stressed? Here are what we think are the top five stressors:

1. Perpetual distraction

The persistent beeping, vibrating and flashing of notifications mean that we are constantly distracted and driven to interrupt what we are doing to check our phones. Indeed, a UK study found that smartphone users unlock their phones on average 85 times a day; and use it for about five hours each day. This means we are unable to focus our attention and consolidate things properly into our memory, causing us to feel more and more 'goldfish-like', which can be quite distressing in itself. This is backed up by research which is beginning to show correlations between high smartphone and internet use, and poor cognitive skills such as attention, memory and learning.

2. Sleep dysregulation

Many of us use our phone at bedtime. You get into bed intending to go to sleep, but you just want to check your phone (just for 'a second') to find out something innocuous like tomorrow's weather... and then an hour later, there you are watching a totally random video, trying to decide whether you hear a computerised voice saying the word 'yanny' or 'laurel'.

Looking at our phones when we should be going to sleep has the double whammy effect of over-stimulating our brains, making it hard to wind down and switch off, and exposing us to blue light from the screen. Research suggests that blue screen exposure can reduce melatonin production, which interrupts our circadian rhythm (i.e. sleep-waking cycles), making it harder for us to fall, and stay, asleep. Unfortunately, poor sleep tends to mean poorer resilience and higher levels of anxiety and stress.

3. Work life balance

While in the past there was often a clear boundary between where work life ended, and home life began... this area is now very much grey. Most of us have our work emails on our phones, making us constantly available and contactable. This makes it very difficult for us to ever truly disengage from work and relax.

4. F.O.M.O.

...Or Fear Of Missing Out is essentially a type of social anxiety that arises from the fear that you are missing out on something; whether it's an event, a work or social opportunity, a communication, or a potential connection, or just something cool and ethereal that you might like to see or be part of. So we want to be connected... 'just in case'. To test this, just ask your friends and family if they've ever considered coming off social media. Like us, they probably have... but the majority probably decide not to, because of FOMO. Ironically, the more connected we are, the more likely we may be to experience FOMO, because it is often caused by the posts we see on social media sites like Facebook leading us to believe our friends and acquaintances are having exciting and/or interesting experiences in our absence.

5. Social comparison

We can't help but compare ourselves to others, and social comparison theory suggests that we use these types of comparisons to evaluate how we think and feel about ourselves. Social media, by its nature, actively encourages social comparison, as it is littered with information that can easily be used as metrics of apparent social success (e.g. friends, likes, shares, followers and so forth). These metrics are problematic in themselves, because if we don't get enough likes to a comment or picture we have posted, or if someone has more likes or friends than us, it can make us feel inferior. Furthermore, the disparity between real life and what people actually post on social media means that we tend to only see an extremely edited 'highlight reel' of other people's lives. This effectively gives the false impression that others lead a more exciting/perfect/interesting life than our own, which, in reality, has its fair share of ups, middles and downs for everyone... increasing the likelihood of negative social comparisons being made, which can have serious consequences on our well-being.

23 May 2018

www.open.edu

Anxiety on rise among the young in social media age

By Robert Booth

The number of young people in the UK who say they do not believe that life is worth living has doubled in the last decade, amid a sense of overwhelming pressure from social media which is driving feelings of inadequacy, new research suggests.

In 2009, only 9% of 16–25–year–olds disagreed with the statement that 'life is really worth living', but that has now risen to 18%. More than a quarter also disagree that their life has a sense of purpose, according to a YouGov survey of 2,162 people for the Prince's Trust, a charity that helps 11–30–year–olds into education, training and work. Youth happiness levels have fallen most sharply over the last decade in respect of relationships with friends and emotional health, the survey found, while satisfaction with issues like money and accommodation have remained steady.

The Prince's Trust has been gauging youth opinion for ten years and found that just under half of young people who use social media now feel more anxious about their future when they compare themselves to others on sites and apps such as Instagram, Twitter and Facebook. A similar amount agree that social media makes them feel 'inadequate'. More than half (57%) think social media creates 'overwhelming pressure' to succeed.

The gloomy view on life being taken by a growing minority of young people comes amid reports of an increased rate of teenage suicide. It was reported on Sunday that official statistics due later this year will show that suicides now occur at more than five in 100,000 teenagers in England. That contrasts with a figure of just over three in 100,000 in 2010.

'Social media has become omnipresent in the lives of young people and this research suggests it is exacerbating what is already an uncertain and emotionally turbulent time,' said Nick Stace, UK chief executive of The Prince's Trust. 'Young people are critical to the future success of this country, but they'll only realise their full potential if they believe in themselves and define success in their own terms. It is therefore a moral and economic imperative that employers, government, charities and wider communities put the needs of young people centre stage.'

There were positive feelings about social media too. A third of people said being on social media makes them feel like they can have a voice for their generation and influence positive change, and more than a quarter said it made them happy. However, playing sport (44%), earning enough money to live how they want (62%) and spending time with family (77%) were more likely to drive happiness. Four out of ten young people said they felt more confident online than they do in person, but that rises to almost half among the youngest age group, 16–18–year–olds. The findings follow public pressure on the government to toughen the

regulation of social media companies, which use algorithms to target users with tailored content. Ministers have asked the chief medical officer, Dame Sally Davies, to draw up advice on social media usage for children amid growing concerns about links between its excessive use and mental health problems among children. Education secretary Damian Hinds, said at the weekend that social media companies have a 'moral duty' to act. He announced that children will have lessons in how to deal with the pressures of social media.

Tskenya Frazer, 24, a habitual Instagram and Twitter user until recently, said she would 'feel bad' about her own life when looking at posts from friends about holidays, work promotions, new cars or homes. It also made her question her body image.

'As soon as I woke up I would be on Instagram, scrolling through,' she said. 'I would be on a page with a girl with the most perfect body.'

'Social media reinforces those feelings of not being good enough, that you're too fat, and that is toxic,' Frazer said. 'Social media doesn't induce those feelings but it heightens them.'

The Prince's Trust creates an index based on happiness and confidence which stood at 73 in 2009. It is now at its lowest level yet at 69.

5 February 2019

Living in a poor area increases the risk of anxiety in women, but not men

***An article from* The Conversation.**

By Olivia Remes

THE CONVERSATION

Women living in the most deprived areas are over 60% more likely to have anxiety as women living in richer areas. However, whether men live in poorer or richer areas seems to make very little difference to their anxiety levels, according to new research we conducted at the University of Cambridge.

The disorder that we looked at in our study of over 18,000 British people was generalised anxiety disorder, which is characterised by excessive uncontrollable worry about a number of life circumstances, from work and finances to relationships and health. The worry could extend to major or minor matters, it could be about anything, and it is very difficult to control.

People with generalised anxiety disorder often think that something negative will happen in the future without this belief being necessarily grounded in reality.

They also suffer from symptoms such as restlessness, insomnia and irritability. They may find it difficult to concentrate on tasks at work or school, and their muscles may feel tense, which can lead to frequent headaches, back pain or joint pain. They might also find it hard to fall or stay asleep at night, and this in turn, can make them feel very tired the next day and impairs their concentration further.

While some studies have looked at the personal factors that can increase the risk of anxiety, such as personal income and education, there is a scarcity of studies looking at the effects it places on mental health.

We do know from research that the residential environment has a significant effect on health more generally. Studies have shown that living in areas characterised by high income inequality can lead to an increased risk of serious medical conditions and even early death.

But what about anxiety?

The findings

Well, now we know. Our study shows that the places which we inhabit can increase our risk of anxiety – but more so for women.

Why is women's mental health more affected by living in deprived areas than men's? A number of reasons can account for this. First, women tend to spend more time in their residential environment, because they are more likely than men to have part-time work, take care of children, and carry out domestic activities, such as grocery shopping. If women spend more time at home and also live in a poor area, then they are more likely to be exposed to the stress and strain associated with living in deprivation.

Second, the sexes seem to be differentially affected by various aspects of their environment.

For example, fear of being assaulted and neighbourhood safety is a particular concern for women. If women think their neighbourhoods or communities are unsafe, they are less likely to go for walks and engage in physical activity.

And engaging in physical activity has been shown to have tremendous benefits for mental health.

Third, being embedded in social networks is particularly important for women's mental health. If women live in a deprived area and perceive their community to be unsafe, they are less likely to reach out to their neighbours and form relationships. This, too, can have a negative impact on their mental health.

Fourth, women and men seem to experience and manifest the effects of stress differently.

Women exposed to stress are more likely to internalise its effects and develop mental health problems, while men who are exposed to stress are more likely to externalise its effects and develop conditions, such as alcohol abuse.

What next?

More research is needed on this, but our findings on area deprivation and anxiety, and the discussion around the possible underlying mechanisms are intriguing. It means that investing in local areas will not benefit men and women living in those places in the same way. And this is important to know at a time of scarce economic resources.

In our research, we also found that it isn't a particular aspect of deprivation that is harmful for women's mental health, rather it is the overall effect of living in deprivation that increases the risk of anxiety in the latter group.

Women are increasingly taking on multiple roles in modern society – many have full-time jobs, and take care of children as well as their elderly parents or relatives. All of this adds to their burden and stress, and even more so if they are living in deprivation.

It is no wonder, then, that living in a poor area is linked to generalised anxiety disorder in women. I think this needs to be considered by policy makers and community planners, particularly as the number of women living in deprived circumstances is large worldwide and anxiety is one of the most common mental health conditions today.

5 May 2017

What triggers anxiety? 11 causes that may surprise you

By Kimberly Holland

Overview

Anxiety is a mental health condition that can cause feelings of worry, fear or tension. For some people, anxiety can also cause panic attacks and extreme physical symptoms, like chest pain.

Anxiety disorders are incredibly common. They affect an estimated 40 million people in the United States, according to the Anxiety and Depression Association of America.

What causes anxiety and anxiety disorders can be complicated. It's likely that a combination of factors, including genetics and environmental reasons, play a role. However, it's clear that some events, emotions or experiences may cause symptoms of anxiety to begin or may make them worse. These elements are called triggers.

Anxiety triggers can be different for each person, but many triggers are common among people with these conditions. Most people find they have multiple triggers. But for some people, anxiety attacks can be triggered for no reason at all.

For that reason, it's important to discover any anxiety triggers that you may have. Identifying your triggers is an important step in managing them. Keep reading to learn about these anxiety triggers and what you can do to manage your anxiety.

Anxiety triggers

1. Health issues

A health diagnosis that's upsetting or difficult, such as cancer or a chronic illness, may trigger anxiety or make it worse. This type of trigger is very powerful because of the immediate and personal feelings it produces.

You can help reduce anxiety caused by health issues by being proactive and engaged with your doctor. Talking with a therapist may also be useful, as they can help you learn to manage your emotions around your diagnosis.

2. Medications

Certain prescription and over-the-counter (OTC) medications may trigger symptoms of anxiety. That's because active ingredients in these medications may make you feel uneasy or unwell. Those feelings can set off a series of events in your mind and body that may lead to additional symptoms of anxiety.

Medicines that may trigger anxiety include:

◆ birth control pills

◆ cough and congestion medications

◆ weight loss medications.

Talk with your doctor about how these drugs make you feel and look for an alternative that doesn't trigger your anxiety or worsen your symptoms.

3. Caffeine

Many people rely on their morning cup of joe to wake up, but it might actually trigger or worsen anxiety. According to one study in 2010, people with panic disorder and social anxiety disorder are especially sensitive to the anxiety-inducing effects of caffeine.

Work to cut back your caffeine intake by substituting noncaffeinated options whenever possible.

4. Skipping meals

When you don't eat, your blood sugar may drop. That can lead to jittery hands and a rumbling tummy. It can also trigger anxiety.

Eating balanced meals is important for many reasons. It provides you with energy and important nutrients. If you can't make time for three meals a day, healthy snacks are a great way to prevent low blood sugar, feelings of nervousness or agitation, and anxiety. Remember, food can affect your mood.

5. Negative thinking

Your mind controls much of your body, and that's certainly true with anxiety. When you're upset or frustrated, the words you say to yourself can trigger greater feelings of anxiety.

If you tend to use a lot of negative words when thinking about yourself, learning to refocus your language and feelings when you start down this path is helpful. Working with a therapist can be incredibly helpful with this process.

6. Financial concerns

Worries about saving money or having debt can trigger anxiety. Unexpected bills or money fears are triggers, too.

Learning to manage these types of triggers may require seeking professional help, such as from a financial advisor. Feeling you have a companion and a guide in the process may ease your concern.

7. Parties or social events

If a room full of strangers doesn't sound like fun, you're not alone. Events that require you to make small talk or interact with people you don't know can trigger feelings of anxiety, which may be diagnosed as social anxiety disorder.

To help ease your worries or unease, you can always bring along a companion when possible. But it's also important to work with a professional to find coping mechanisms that make these events more manageable in the long term.

8. Conflict

Relationship problems, arguments, disagreements – these conflicts can all trigger or worsen anxiety. If conflict particularly triggers you, you may need to learn conflict resolution strategies. Also, talk with a therapist or other mental health expert to learn how to manage the feelings these conflicts cause.

9. Stress

Daily stressors like traffic jams or missing your train can cause anyone anxiety. But long-term or chronic stress can lead to long-term anxiety and worsening symptoms, as well as other health problems.

Stress can also lead to behaviours like skipping meals, drinking alcohol, or not getting enough sleep. These factors can trigger or worsen anxiety, too.

Treating and preventing stress often requires learning coping mechanisms. A therapist or counsellor can help you learn to recognise your sources of stress and handle them when they become overwhelming or problematic.

10. Public events or performances

Public speaking, talking in front of your boss, performing in a competition, or even just reading aloud is a common trigger of anxiety. If your job or hobbies require this, your doctor or therapist can work with you to learn ways to be more comfortable in these settings.

Also, positive reinforcements from friends and colleagues can help you feel more comfortable and confident.

11. Personal triggers

These triggers may be difficult to identify, but a mental health specialist is trained to help you identify them. These may begin with a smell, a place, or even a song. Personal triggers remind you, either consciously or unconsciously, of a bad memory or traumatic event in your life. Individuals with post-traumatic stress disorder (PTSD) frequently experience anxiety triggers from environmental triggers.

Identifying personal triggers may take time, but it's important so you can learn to overcome them.

Tips for identifying triggers

If you can identify and understand your triggers, you can work to avoid them and to cope. You can learn specific coping strategies to handle the triggers when they happen.

Here are three tips for identifying triggers:

- **Start a journal.** Write down when your anxiety is noticeable and record what you think might have led to the trigger. Some apps can help you track your anxiety, too.

- **Work with a therapist.** Some anxiety triggers can be difficult to identify, but a mental health specialist has training that can help you. They may use talk therapy, journaling, or other methods to find triggers.

- **Be honest with yourself.** Anxiety can cause negative thoughts and poor self-assessments. This can make identifying triggers difficult because of the anxious reactions. Be patient with yourself and be willing to explore things in your past to identify how they may affect you today.

Symptoms of anxiety

The most common symptoms of anxiety include:

- uncontrollable worry
- fear
- muscle tension
- a fast heartbeat

- difficulty sleeping or insomnia
- difficulty concentrating
- physical discomfort
- tingling
- restlessness
- feeling on edge
- irritability.

If you experience these symptoms regularly for six months or more, you may have generalised anxiety disorder (GAD). Other types of anxiety disorders exist as well. The symptoms for those may be different than GAD. For example, with panic disorder you may experience:

- a rapid heartbeat or palpitations
- sweating
- trembling
- shaking
- feeling as if your throat is closing.

Seeking help

If you believe you worry too much or suspect you have an anxiety disorder, it's time to seek help. Recognising the anxiety is often difficult because the symptoms become common over time.

'Occasional anxiety is common, but chronic feelings of worry, fear or dread aren't. They're a sign you should seek professional help.'

Start the discussion by talking with your doctor. They'll discuss your symptoms, conduct a health history, and do a physical exam. They'll want to rule out any possible physical problems that may be causing the issues, too.

From there, your doctor may choose to treat you with medication. They may also refer you to a mental health specialist, such as a psychologist or psychiatrist. These doctors can use a combination of talk therapy and medication to treat anxiety and prevent triggers.

Takeaway

Occasional anxiety is common, but chronic feelings of worry, fear or dread aren't common. They're a sign you should seek professional help. The good news is that anxiety is a highly treatable mental health condition. However, many people with anxiety don't seek treatment.

Eight symptoms of social anxiety

Social anxiety can leave us feeling intensely fearful and awkward in, and of, social situations. It can have a massive impact on our day-to-day lives too and influence our interactions with other people, affecting relationships and sometimes too, our work. The anxiety often doesn't end when the socialising ends either, we may find that we ruminate over things we've said or not said, things we did or didn't do. There's an acute sense of being judged, appearing rude, aloof or flaky, and of never really fitting in. We might find that we avoid social situations as much as possible which can lead to us feeling lonely and isolated. Where we can't avoid the social situation, we might find that we constantly go over and over what we might do or say in response to certain situations and conversations. It's exhausting.

Physical symptoms

There are loads of physical symptoms that we could encounter if we're living with social anxiety. These could include things like feeling sick, sweating, having palpitations, blushing, shaking, feeling dizzy, feeling faint and diarrhoea.

All these things can be due to anxiety putting our body in overdrive. These symptoms can feel embarrassing, and this embarrassment can increase our anxiety and make them even worse. It can be a vicious circle.

Fear

When we live with social anxiety, we can often feel gripped with fear. It can root us to the spot, cause us to tense up and might make it hard to move or speak. We might feel as though our heart is racing. Because we're so tense, our muscles can begin to ache, which can be really painful.

All of the 'what ifs' can swirl around our heads, tying us in knots. It can cause us to feel trapped and to panic.

Self-consciousness

Excessive self-consciousness can take hold, particularly when we are in social situations. We might live in baggy or dark coloured clothes to try and blend in. It can feel impossible to keep eye contact with the people we're speaking to. We might find ourselves hiding behind our hair. Our speech can become quiet because we don't want to draw attention to ourselves or we might talk at a rate of knots because we feel so nervous. There are times when we might wish that we could just disappear. Often we are painfully aware of how much space we take up – both physically and with any noise or movements we make.

Intense worry

Upcoming social events can cause havoc with the social anxiety we experience. They can cause us to feel intense worry. This could range from worrying hours before an event to days, weeks, or even months. We could be worrying about anything and everything. What to wear, who might be there, what they might say. How we should respond. Whether we will look or say something inappropriate. Whether we'll fit in. How we might get out of it.

Whether we'll be able to escape if we need to… it can be a never-ending list.

Avoidance

Because of the anxiety that social situations can bring up, we often avoid them. This can limit the things that we do feel able to take part in. It can mean that we miss out on events and get-togethers that we really want to go to. We might not see our friends or family as often as we'd like to. It's not that we're anti-social or dislike our loved ones, it's just that the thought of social situations can make us feel so unwell that going to them feels impossible.

Negative thoughts

Social anxiety can cause us to have extremely negative thoughts about ourselves. Even if we receive ten positive comments, and one mediocre comment, we will take the mediocre comment as a negative and run with it. We often have very low self-confidence and don't think much of ourselves. We can feel like such a burden. Often we might think that people don't really want us around and are just 'putting up with us'. Conversations we've had can play on our mind for weeks on end as we wonder if we got it 'right', or if we said/did something silly. These negative thoughts can overwhelm any positives we might feel about ourselves. The more we think them, the lower our confidence sinks, the lower our confidence sinks, the more negative thoughts we have.

Safety behaviours

Safety behaviours can help us to manage social situations and help us to manage the symptoms of social anxiety. This could include things like making sure we always have someone with us. Knowing how we'll get home. Choosing to spend less time in larger groups and preferring smaller gatherings. Wearing headphones to drown out the external noise.

Some safety behaviours, like making sure we always have something in our pocket that we can fiddle with, can be really helpful. Others, like needing to rely on alcohol to manage certain occasions, might not be so helpful in the long term.

Struggling to do things with others watching

Lots of us will find that we struggle to do things if there is anyone watching us. This could include things like making a phone call, eating lunch, or printing something at work. It could be the panic about walking into a venue on our own, putting our hand up to ask a question at an event, holding in a cough because we don't want everyone to look our way, or needing the loo whilst on a train but not wanting to walk through so many people.

Social anxiety is so much more than 'shyness' and it's typically where fear of social situations is long-lasting and disruptive. It's a fairly common condition that starts to affect us in our teenage years and is treatable with the right help and support.

4 October 2018

Mental health: depression and anxiety in young mothers is up by 50% in a generation

THE CONVERSATION

An article from **The Conversation**

By Rebecca Pearson, Lecturer in Psychiatric Epidemiology, University of Bristol

Back when it first started, 17% of young pregnant women in the Children of the 90s study reported symptoms severe enough to indicate clinical levels of depression. This figure was already worryingly high in the 1990s, but in their daughters' generation it is even more common: 25% of the second generation of the study – women under the age of 24 who are becoming pregnant now – are reporting signs of depression and anxiety.

Children of the 90s started following the mental and physical health of families in the UK in the 1990s. The young mothers who responded were not reporting that they had depression or were seeking help. Rather, the women answered questions anonymously about how they had been feeling over the previous two weeks. The questions were never changed, so that women responding in the 1990s answered the same questions about their lives as their daughter's generation in the 2010s. This means that many of the women who took part will have had clinical depression or anxiety without actually recognising it as such.

In a study published in *The Lancet*, colleagues and I suggested too that far too many young women are suffering. And there are also implications for the unborn baby.

How antenatal depression affects babies

We know that depression and anxiety in mothers can have an influence on their child at any point in the child's life. Arguably, however, antenatal depression – which occurs during pregnancy – is the period of greatest risk to the child.

While pregnant, the stress hormones and other physiological consequences of depression and anxiety that circulate in the mother's system are also picked up by the developing foetus, through the placenta and in the womb. This can alter the way a baby's stress system develops.

Depression during and after pregnancy comes at a critical time for the baby. It can make it more difficult for the mother to interact with her baby, especially during times when the infant is distressed. Depressed ways of thinking and behaving may get picked up by the child in an ongoing cycle of learnt behaviour.

What's behind the increase?

It's very difficult to prove what may have led to an increase in young pregnant women feeling this way. However, when trying to understand rises in anxiety and depression we can look to what has changed across the generations.

It's possible that this new generation of pregnant women are more comfortable talking about their emotions and better able to answer the questions accurately. In this case, it doesn't negate the fact that 25% of young pregnant women today are depressed, but it may suggest that in the 1990s it was similarly high but women were less able or willing to express it.

However, there have been two key changes in the living standards of young mothers in the last three decades that could have caused a genuine increase in depression.

There has been a substantial increase in working motherhood since the 1990s, with more young women reaching higher levels of education and wanting a career. The increasing cost of living and soaring house prices mean that there is little choice for most and two incomes from a

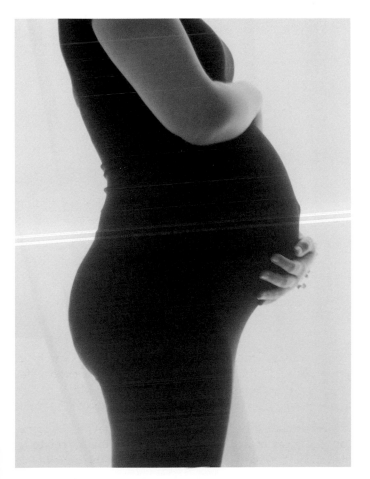

woman and her partner is the norm. The physical burden of working while pregnant, the financial pressures of often uncertain maternity pay, and the psychological impact of expecting the perfect career and family are all likely to have taken their toll. Partners also play a vital role in sharing this burden and can also need support.

The generation entering motherhood now will have also been the first to grow up alongside social media. When Facebook launched in 2004, the children born at the start of the study were in their early teens. This generation of young mothers will have been inundated with more information and social comparisons as they enter their first pregnancy, and it has been suggested that the potential stigma and social isolation of being a young pregnant mum may be exacerbated by social media.

Tackling antenatal depression

It's important that research like this isn't used to blame mothers, and increase the already burdensome guilt attached to motherhood. It should instead be used to support families that need help. There is growing evidence that suggests the risks to the child from antenatal depression are not inevitable and can be buffered by positive environments and supportive families and communities.

Antenatal depression is routinely screened for by midwives, as recommended by national guidelines. However, in most areas, nowhere near as many women who indicate high levels of symptoms in these types of surveys actually come forward to get help from midwives or GPs.

This may be because women don't identify with the label of depression. The symptoms which were driving the increase in poor mental health in our study were reported feelings of fear and being overwhelmed. Currently, guidelines suggest that midwives should consider asking about anxiety as an optional suggestion, but our study found that this may be very important to ask. Discussions around emotions or whatever women feel comfortable with, rather than terms like depression, could help more women come forward.

However, the issue remains that if depression and anxiety is more common among young mothers, it's likely that there are a lot more women out there to support than specialist services can cope with. There are just not enough resources. As well as more funding for such services, there needs to be support within the community. Perhaps it is also time to talk about how modern life might need to change to support young women, before this rise in antenatal depression takes its toll on the next generation too.

6 August 2018

Anxiety treatments

Self-help resources

A self-help resource might be the first treatment option your doctor offers you. This is because it's available quite quickly, and there's a chance it could help you to feel better without needing to try other options.

Self-help could be delivered through:

◆ **Workbooks.** For example, your GP might recommend particular titles from a scheme called Reading Well Books on Prescription. This scheme is supported by most local libraries, so you can go and check the books out for free – you don't actually need a prescription from a doctor.

◆ **A computer-based CBT program** for treating anxiety, panic and phobias, such as FearFighter. FearFighter costs money if you use it privately, but in some areas it's free to use on the NHS with a referral from your GP.

You might be offered a resource to work through your own, or on a course with other people who experience similar difficulties.

Talking treatments

If self-help resources aren't likely to help with the anxiety problems you're experiencing, or you've already tried them and they haven't helped, your doctor should offer you a talking treatment. There are two types of talking treatment recommended for anxiety and panic:

◆ **Cognitive behavioural therapy (CBT)** – this focuses on how your thoughts, beliefs and attitudes affect your feelings and behaviour, and teaches you coping skills for dealing with different problems.

◆ **Applied relaxation therapy** – this involves learning how to relax your muscles in situations where you normally experience anxiety.

Medication

Your doctor might offer to prescribe you medication to help manage some symptoms. Some people find it helpful to try talking treatments and medication at the same time, but medication shouldn't be the only thing you're offered.

Medications you might be offered include:

◆ **Antidepressants.** Usually this will be a type called a selective serotonin reuptake inhibitor (SSRI), but these drugs can sometimes cause side effects such as sleeping problems or feeling more anxious than you did before. If SSRIs don't work or aren't suitable, you may be offered a different kind called a tricyclic antidepressant.

◆ **Pregabalin.** In some cases, such as if you have a diagnosis of generalised anxiety disorder (GAD), your doctor may decide to prescribe you a drug called pregabalin. This is an antiseizure drug which is normally used to treat epilepsy (a neurological disorder that can cause seizures), but is also licensed to treat anxiety.

◆ **Beta-blockers.** Beta-blockers are sometimes used to treat the physical symptoms of anxiety, such as a rapid heartbeat, palpitations and tremors (shaking). However, they are not psychiatric drugs so they don't reduce any of the psychological symptoms. They may be helpful in certain situations, such as if you have to face a phobia.

◆ **Benzodiazepine tranquillisers.** If you experience very severe anxiety that is having a significant impact on your day-to-day life, you may be offered a benzodiazepine tranquilliser. But these drugs can cause unpleasant side effects and can become addictive, so your doctor should only prescribe them at a low dose for a short time, to help you through a crisis period.

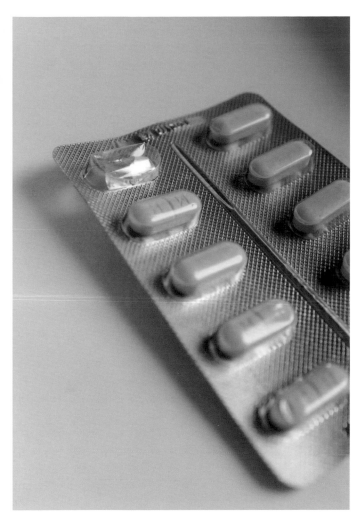

Before deciding to take any drug, it's important to make sure you have all the facts you need to make an informed choice.

How do I access treatment?

To get treatment on the NHS, the first step is normally to visit your doctor (also known as your GP). They will do an assessment, which might include asking you to fill in a questionnaire about how often you feel worried, anxious and nervous. They should then explain your treatment options to you, and you can decide together what might suit you best.

Unfortunately, NHS waiting lists for talking treatments can be very long. If you're finding it hard to access talking treatments you could consider:

◆ **Charities and specialist organisations.**

◆ **Private therapy.** Finding a private therapist is another option some people choose to explore, but it's not suitable for everyone because it can be expensive.

What if my anxiety stops me from seeking help?

It can be especially hard to access treatment if making or attending an appointment with your doctor involves doing something that causes anxiety for you. For example, you might not feel able to talk on the phone or leave the house.

Here are some things you could try:

• Ask your doctor if they offer home visits or telephone assessments. If not, they might be able to book you an appointment at a time when the surgery tends to be quiet.

• Some GP practices will allow someone else to ring up and book appointments for you (with your consent). It could also help to have someone come with you to the appointment for support.

• Depending on what's available in your area, you may be able to refer yourself for talking treatment at a local Improving Access to Psychological Therapies (IAPT) service. Some IAPT services are delivered over the phone. You can search for IAPT services on the NHS Choices website.

You can read the National Institute for Health and Care Excellence (NICE) best-practice guidelines for treating anxiety disorders in full in English or Welsh on the NICE website.

If you don't know what is wrong with you, how do you know how to fix it? For me, actually being diagnosed with anxiety and panic disorder came as a relief! It meant that I wasn't imagining the awful symptoms I'd been experiencing.

What if I don't feel better?

Your doctor should offer you regular appointments to check how you're doing, and see how well any treatment is working for you. Different things work for different people, so if a particular medication or talking treatment doesn't work for you, your doctor should offer an alternative.

If you've tried a range of treatments and none of them have helped, your doctor might refer you to a community mental health team (CMHT). This is is made up of a number of different healthcare professionals, such as psychiatrists and clinical psychologists. Your CMHT can assess you separately and offer you a personalised treatment plan.

This is particularly recommended if:

• your symptoms are making it very difficult to carry out everyday activities

• you have a serious physical health problem or another mental health problem

• you're having thoughts of self-harm or suicide.

It's important to remember that recovery is a journey, and it won't always be straightforward. You might find it more helpful to focus on learning more about yourself and developing ways to cope, rather than trying to get rid of every symptom of your anxiety problem.

This information was published in September 2017 – to be revised in 2020.

Developing teen brains are vulnerable to anxiety – but treatment can help

An article from **The Conversation.**

By Paola Odriozola, Ph.D. Student in Psychology and Dylan Gee, Assistant Professor of Psycholgy, Yale University

THE CONVERSATION

Adolescence is the life stage when mental illnesses are most likely to emerge, with anxiety disorders being the most common. Recent estimates suggest that over 30% of teens have an anxiety disorder. That means about one of every three teenagers is struggling with anxiety that significantly interferes with their life and is unlikely to fade without treatment.

Kayla is the anxious teen protagonist in the recent movie *Eighth Grade*. From the acne peeking out through her make-up to the frequent 'likes' that punctuate her speech, she seems to be a quintessentially awkward teen. Inside her mind, though, the realities of social anxiety meet the typical storm and stress of adolescence. Through its warm yet heart-wrenchingly truthful portrayal of an awkward and anxious teen, *Eighth Grade* provides a relatable character for identifying and understanding how teen anxiety can really look and feel.

As developmental neuroscientists, watching the film sparked a conversation about the latest science on anxiety during adolescence. Researchers are learning more about why the teenage brain is so vulnerable to anxiety – and developing effective treatments that are increasingly available.

What does teen anxiety look like?

The hallmark of anxiety disorders is fear or nervousness that does not go away, even in the absence of any real threat. In an emotional scene, Kayla shares that she's 'really, like, nervous all the time' and she '[tries] really hard not to feel that way', as if she's constantly waiting to ride a roller coaster with butterflies in her stomach, but never getting the relief of the ride ending.

For teens and parents, it can be hard to disentangle normal emotional changes that often accompany puberty from anxiety that may require professional care. Some of Kayla's worries and fears are highly typical – feeling nervous about what others will think, worrying about making friends, wanting to 'fit in'. The problem is that, unlike everyday worry, Kayla experiences these feelings all the time and in ways that force her to miss out on important opportunities of adolescence like exploring relationships.

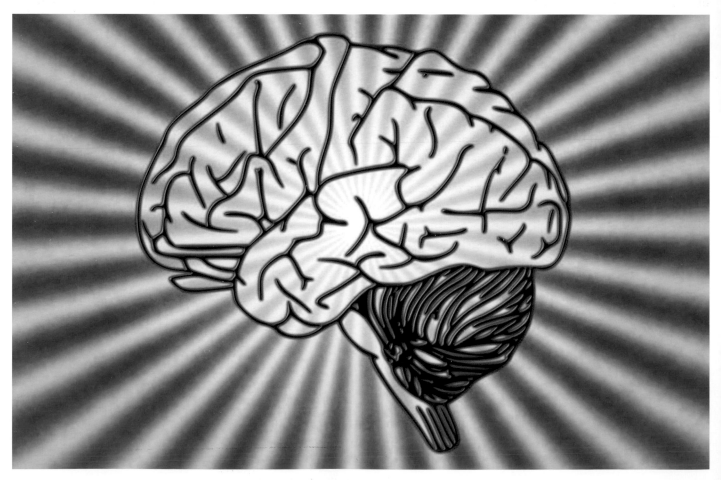

anxiety to gradually and repeatedly expose themselves to the very situations that they fear.

A socially anxious teen might start with imagining sending a classmate a text asking to hang out, gradually move on to sending that text, or even calling a classmate on the phone, and eventually initiating a conversation with an unfamiliar peer at a party. The goal is to practise these anxiety-provoking actions and associate them with a new state of safety.

Decades of studies in animals and people have helped psychology researchers understand more about how the brain regulates fear. Building on this work, emerging neuroscience evidence suggests that current treatments for anxiety directly modify the same amygdala-prefrontal connections that are in flux during adolescence and implicated in anxiety.

For example, evidence suggests that both cognitive behavioural therapy and medication treatment with selective serotonin reuptake inhibitors (SSRIs) may reduce amygdala reactivity and enhance prefrontal control. The treatments help these brain circuits regulate fear and keep them from overreacting to potentially anxiety-provoking situations.

Studies on the teenage brain are increasingly revealing why adolescence may be such a vulnerable time for anxiety. Researchers have focused on connections between the brain's limbic system, including the amygdala which governs emotion, and the prefrontal cortex, the frontmost part of the brain. These connections are essential for controlling emotions, including fear, a core symptom in anxiety disorders.

The problem is that these amygdala-prefrontal cortex connections are slow to develop; they continue to strengthen into one's early 20s. During adolescence, the brain goes through rapid changes in its shape and size and also in how it works. The very structures and connections in the brain that help to manage emotions are in flux during this developmental period, making teens especially vulnerable to stress and anxiety.

Anxious teens are at heightened risk for a host of long-term problems, including depression, substance abuse and suicide.

Evidence-based treatments work

Fortunately, help exists for anxious teens. As is the case for the startlingly high 80% of youth struggling with anxiety who don't get treatment, Kayla's journey through *Eighth Grade* also does not include any professional help. Yet no teen should need to face anxiety on their own. Psychotherapy and medications can both be highly effective.

Cognitive behavioural therapy (CBT) is one of the most effective and widely used psychosocial treatments for anxiety in teens. In CBT, therapists help individuals with

Researchers like us are actively working to leverage growing insight into the teenage brain to further optimise anxiety-focused treatments. Neuroscientific studies have the unique advantage of peering inside the teenage brain to directly assess developmental changes in amygdala prefrontal cortex connections. Using imaging technologies, we're able to characterise the state of this neural circuitry and how well it's controlling fear at a given stage of development. And this knowledge provides clues about how to match up the most effective behavioural techniques for regulating anxiety with a particular teen's stage of brain circuit development.

Evidence suggests that the ways in which people learn about potential dangers in their environment and how they are able to control or regulate responses to those threats undergo important changes during the teenage years. Translating this knowledge into the treatment realm could provide new windows into precision medicine, allowing treatments to be tailored specifically for teenagers.

Although the teenage brain is prone to anxiety because of where it is on its path of biological development, effective treatment options exist and are continually being refined to target the adolescent brain.

2 November 2018

Autistic people listen to their hearts to test anti-anxiety therapy

Trial seeks further proof that tuning into our internal organs' activity can reduce anxiety.

By Hannah Devlin, Science correspondent

A pioneering therapy aimed at lowering anxiety by tuning into your own heartbeat is being put to the test in the first clinical trial of its kind.

The treatment, known as interoception-directed therapy, is being tested on 120 autistic people, for whom anxiety is a common problem.

The trial follows a decade's research by Prof. Sarah Garfinkel, a psychologist at the University of Sussex, into the intriguing ways that interactions between the heart and the brain influence emotions and behaviour. The latest work, funded by the mental health charity MQ: Transforming Mental Health, aims to turn these insights into a therapy.

'Anxiety is really high in the autistic population,' said Garfinkel. '50% of people with autism also potentially have anxiety, which is so high and really not known.'

The ability to tune into the activity of our internal organs is called interoception and there is emerging evidence that this ability is linked to how well a person is able to identify their own emotional state and to empathise with others.

Garfinkel believes that altered interoception may be a factor in why autistic people experience the world differently. Her work has shown that autistic people tend to find it far harder to detect their own heartbeats – and the worse they are at this task, the greater their anxiety tends to be.

The 120 trial participants are being asked to complete eight training sessions over several weeks. During training, their heartbeat is tracked using a pulse oximeter and they are asked to 'listen in' to their heart and count how many beats occur in a set time period. They are then given the correct answer and the exercise is repeated.

A pilot study involving participants without autism showed the training improved people's interoceptive awareness and significantly reduced anxiety levels.

Becka, a 41-year-old from Brighton, who was diagnosed as autistic as an adult, is one of the trial participants. 'I don't really remember a time I wasn't anxious,' she said. 'It seems [to be] always there in the background … and at times I have felt taken over by my anxiety.'

Becka struggles to manage sensory overload, saying the world sometimes feels 'intense, loud, fast, painful', which she said contributes to feelings of stress and anxiety. Focusing on her heart and breathing is something she has learned

to do naturally as a coping strategy and she enjoyed the training. 'It was good to tune in and focus on my heartbeat,' she said. 'No matter how busy outside or inside is, I can still focus on that.' Garfinkel's interest was sparked after reading a scientific paper on autism and empathy.

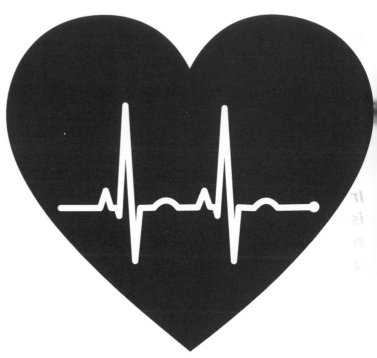

'I found within this paper an almost buried graph showing that if you measure the bodily response of someone with autism to seeing someone in pain, it's actually greater,' said Garfinkel. 'They have a heightened bodily response to the pain of others.'

This finding runs counter to the idea that autistic people 'lack empathy', she said. 'Early accounts of autism sometimes said they didn't have empathy and for me that's really not true at all,' she said.

However, autistic people can feel disconnected from their own emotions and struggle to assess what people around them are feeling.

'It made me wonder, if they're having this very heightened bodily response, is there something altered about their interoception, their capacity to sense and use these signals?'

One hypothesis is that, in autistic people, empathetic responses are occurring at the brain's fast, instinctive level, reflected by changes in heartbeat. However, the brain may be less adept at interpreting these signals and so having these constant unexplained increases in heart rate could potentially leave people feeling under threat, causing anxiety.

Garfinkel hopes the latest trial could provide further insights into whether the hypothesis, which is under active debate in the field, is correct. The participants will also have brain scans before and after training to look for any potential changes in a brain area called the insula, which picks up signals from the heart and is also involved in emotion.

Sophie Dix, director of research at MQ: Transforming Mental Health, said: 'This project has so much potential to inform treatments and further understanding of anxiety in autistic people. Research like this provides hope for better treatments for mental health kindled by our increased understanding of the link between the mind and the body.'

How to test your own interoceptive awareness

1) Find a quiet place.

2) Set a timer for one minute.

3) Close your eyes and try to detect your heartbeat. When you're ready, start the timer and try to count your heartbeats for a minute.

4) Repeat the exercise, but this time feeling your pulse to take an accurate reading of your heart rate.

Tip: if you're struggling to tune into your heartbeat, try running up and down some stairs or doing star jumps until your heart pounds and then try to stick with it as it returns to normal.

14 December 2018

How your imagination can help you overcome your fears

In your imagination, you can do anything. Riding a dragon? Piece of cake. Imagination is what fuels creativity and allows us to come up with innovative solutions. New research assessing brain scans shows that our imagination can also help us get rid of our anxieties and fears.

By Maria Cohut

Your imagination is a powerful tool that you could use to overcome your fears. Our imagination is an incredibly useful tool. It can soothe us during difficult times and help us solve problems, create new things, and consider possible courses of action.

Some researchers have argued that our imagination, which gives us the ability to consider different scenarios, is at the core of what makes humans different from the rest of the animal kingdom.

Moreover, existing research has suggested that what we imagine can actually affect our minds and bodies in very concrete ways.

For instance, a study that the journal *Psychological Science* published in 2009 found that when we imagine doing something, our minds and bodies anticipate the imagined action as though it were a real action.

The results of another study, which featured in *Current Biology* in 2013, suggest that imagining that we hear certain sounds or see particular shapes can change how we perceive the world in real time.

New research by a team from the University of Colorado Boulder and the Icahn School of Medicine at Mount Sinai in New York, NY, now proves that what we imagine can seem just as real to our brains as actual experiences.

As the investigators explain in their study paper, which appears in the journal *Neuron* we can harness the 'magical powers' of our imagination to help us overcome persistent fears and anxiety disorders.

'This research confirms that imagination is a neurological reality that can impact our brains bodies in ways that matter for our wellbeing,' says Prof. Tor Wager, co-senior author of the study.

The power of what you imagine

When it comes to helping people address their phobias or anxiety disorders, psychologists may recommend 'exposure therapy.' This approach aims to desensitise a person to stimuli that trigger a fear response by repeatedly exposing them to these stimuli in a completely safe environment.

This can help a person disassociate those stimuli from a sense of threat and impending negative consequences.

In the new study, the researchers used functional MRI to scan participants' brains and assess brain activity both in real and imagined situations involving unpleasant triggers. The aim was to see whether and how imagination may help us discard negative associations.

'These novel findings bridge a long-standing gap between clinical practice and cognitive neuroscience,' notes the study's lead author Marianne Cumella Reddan, who is a graduate student in the Department of Psychology and Neuroscience at the University of Colorado Boulder.

'This is the first neuroscience study to show that imagining a threat can actually alter the way it is represented in the brain,' she adds.

In the current study, the research team recruited 68 healthy participants, whom they conditioned to associate a particular sound with receiving an electric shock that was uncomfortable but not painful.

They then split the participants into three groups. To those in the first group, the researchers played the sound that the participants now associated with an unpleasant physical experience.

Those in the second group had to imagine hearing that same sound instead, while those in the third group – the controls – had to imagine pleasant sounds, such as the trills of birds and the pitter-patter of rain. None of the participants received any further electric shocks.

Imagining a threat repeatedly can help

While the volunteers were either hearing the triggering sound, imagining it, or imagining a pleasant sound, the researchers assessed their brain activity using functional MRI. The team also measured their physiological responses by placing sensors on their skin.

The investigators found that brain activity was very similar in the participants who actually heard the threatening sound and those who only imagined hearing it.

In all of these volunteers, the auditory cortex (the brain region that processes sound), the nucleus accumbens (associated with learned fear) and the ventromedial prefrontal cortex (which signals exposure to risk) became active.

However, after the participants repeatedly heard or imagined hearing the triggering sound without receiving the expected electric shock, they stopped being afraid. The process had extinguished the association between that sound and an unpleasant experience. This phenomenon is known as 'extinction'.

In the control group, in which the participants had imagined pleasant sounds only, other brain regions lit up in the functional MRI scans, and the negative association between the triggering sound and the electric shock never went away.

'Statistically, real and imagined exposure to the threat were not different at the whole brain level, and imagination worked just as well,' explains Reddan.

> '*I think a lot of people assume that the way to reduce fear or negative emotion is to imagine something good. In fact, what might be more effective is exactly the opposite: imagining the threat, but without the negative consequences.*'
>
> *– Prof. Tor Wager*

You can 'update' bad memories

The researchers also suggest that, thanks to the power of imagination, we may even be able to 'revise' and 'update' memories that are unpleasant or unhelpful.

'If you have a memory that is no longer useful for you or is crippling you, you can use imagination to tap into it, change it, and re-consolidate it, updating the way you think about and experience something,' says Reddan.

However, just how vivid each of our imaginations is may affect the outcome of such experiments. Thus, the investigators explain, those with particularly vivid imaginations may benefit the most from 'manipulating' unpleasant associations, while those with less-active imaginations may not see much of a difference.

There is a real need for more research into the powers of imagination, say the researchers, but the current findings emphasise one thing – namely, that we should not underestimate the effect of what we imagine.

'Manage your imagination and what you permit yourself to imagine,' encourages Prof. Wager. 'You can use imagination constructively to shape what your brain learns from experience,' he adds.

12 December 2018

Mentoring can reduce anxiety, study finds

Mentoring of junior colleagues can reduce anxiety and improve the mental health of the mentors themselves, finds a new study.

Funnily enough, this will help us both.

The mentoring of junior colleagues can reduce anxiety and improve the mental health of the mentors themselves in high-pressure occupations, concludes a new study co-authored at Cambridge Judge Business School involving an English police force.

While previous research had indicated that the anxiety of mentees can be reduced through the guidance of more senior mentors, the new study finds that imparting knowledge and experience can also help mentors by making their jobs more rewarding.

'We found that mentoring relationships provide a unique context for mentors to discuss and normalise their concerns, to share ideas for managing anxieties, and to find more meaning in their work,' concludes the study, published in the *Journal of Vocational Behavior*.

'Mentoring relationships appeared to provide an organisational mechanism to prompt supervisor and colleague interactions, which in turn facilitated a reduction in the mentors' anxiety.'

In England alone, mental illness accounts for annual expenditure on healthcare of £14 billion and a reduction in gross domestic product of £52 billion owing to people unable to work to their full capacity.

Policing was chosen as an appropriate setting to study how mentoring can reduce anxiety in occupations that play important social roles, including the medical profession and the military – roles that require mental strength in challenging situations coupled with political pressure

to become more efficient. The study follows a mentoring programme that was rolled out at one of 43 territory-based police forces in England and Wales since 2013.

Despite the pressures of their roles – including threats, abuse, snap decisions and the risk of death – police officers tend not to seek support from other officers, including more senior colleagues, to avoid 'negative stigma' associated with mental health disorders. Mentoring can help fill this void, the study says.

"The study suggests that a relatively inexpensive practice such as mentoring can help reduce anxiety among both senior and junior staff, and this could help organisations address the serious and costly workplace issues of anxiety and mental health,' says study co-author Dr Thomas Roulet, University Senior Lecturer in Organisation Theory at Cambridge Judge Business School. "While the study focused on high-stress roles in the public eye, we believe that the findings may also apply to other occupations that also have anxiety-provoking pressures."

The study is co-authored by Dr Michael Gill of Said Business School at Oxford University and Chief Inspector Stephen Kerridge of the Cambridgeshire Constabulary.

Excerpts of interviews with mentors and mentees indicated that it was beneficial for people in such busy and often frantic jobs as policing to have an opportunity to be 'listened to' and to take note of the fact that 'we've all gone through' certain work experiences.

'Mentoring provided reassurance to the mentors by illuminating how other, often junior officers also experience anxiety thereby normalising their own experiences,' the study says.

'By acknowledging that anxieties are common, both the mentees and mentors in this study appeared to be more comfortable discussing such issues and therefore in developing different coping mechanisms.'

11 September 2018

Reference: Michael J. Gill et al. 'Mentoring for mental health: A mixed-method study of the benefits of formal mentoring programmes in the English police force.' Journal Of Vocational Behavior (2018). DOI: 10.1016/j.jvb.2018.08.005

Originally published on the Cambridge Judge Business School website.

Lavender really does help you relax and could even treat anxiety, scientists reveal

The purple plant's healing powers for reducing stress are real.

By Sarah Young

The famous relaxing effects of lavender are real and could even be used medically to treat anxiety, new research suggests.

From blooming gardens to aromatherapy oils and bubble baths, people have long claimed that lavender has calming and relaxing benefits.

And now, scientists have confirmed that the smell of the purple plant really does help people unwind.

So much so, that it could even be used to calm patients before surgery, as an alternative to sleeping tablets and to treat anxiety.

Researchers at Kagoshima University in Japan came to this conclusion after analysing whether the smell of linalool, a fragrant alcohol found in lavender extracts, helps mice relax.

They found that mice which were exposed to the aroma did in fact show less signs of anxiety.

'In folk medicine, it has long been believed that odorous compounds derived from plant extracts can relieve anxiety,' co-author Dr Hideki Kashiwadani said.

'As in previous studies, we found that linalool odour has an anxiolytic [anti-anxiety] effect in normal mice.'

Unlike sedative drugs such as benzodiazepines, which can affect a person's movement in a similar way to alcohol, the researchers also noted that smelling linalool did not impair the movement of the mice at all.

However, they did find that mice who had no sense of smell did not benefit from the same anti-anxiety effects, indicating that the relaxation in normal mice was indeed triggered by olfactory signals evoked by linalool odour.

What's more, the anti-anxiety effect in normal mice disappeared when they were pre-treated with flumazenil, which blocks GABAARS – the brain cells' receptors targeted by benzodiazepines.

'When combined, these results suggest that linalool does not act directly on GABAA receptors like benzodiazepines do - but must activate them via olfactory neurons in the nose in order to produce its relaxing effects,' explains Kashiwadani.

'Our study also opens the possibility that relaxation seen in mice fed or injected with linalool could in fact be due to the smell of the compound emitted in their exhaled breath.'

The researchers claim that more studies are now needed to establish the safety and efficacy of linalool administered via different routes before a move to human trials.

Nonetheless, they believe that the findings bring us closer to clinical use of linalool to help relieve anxiety and stress.

The research is published in *Frontiers in Behavioral Neuroscience.*

25 October 2018

Sunny disposition 'helps ward off anxiety and depression'

By Paul Gallagher

Always look on the bright side of life, especially if you want to fend off depression, anxiety and panic disorders it seems.

Perseverance and a sunny disposition acts as a safeguard against mental health problems, according to a study of thousands of Americans over 18 years. Surprisingly, a sense of control did not have an effect on the mental health of participants across time, the research team found.

They used data from 3,294 adults with an average age of 45, nearly all were white and slightly fewer than half were college-educated. Data were collected three times, in 1995 to 1996, 2004 to 2005 and 2012 to 2013.

At each interval, participants were asked to rate their goal persistence, self-mastery and positive reappraisal. Diagnoses for major depressive, anxiety and panic disorders were also collected.

People who showed more goal persistence and optimism during the first assessment in the mid-1990s had greater reductions in depression, anxiety and panic disorders across the 18 years, according to the authors. And throughout those years, people who began with fewer mental health problems showed more increased perseverance toward life goals and were better at focusing on the positive side of unfortunate events.

Purposefulness

'Perseverance cultivates a sense of purposefulness that can create resilience against or decrease current levels of major depressive disorder, generalised anxiety disorder and panic disorder,' said Dr Nur Hani Zainal, from The Pennsylvania State University and lead author of the study.

'Looking on the bright side of unfortunate events has the same effect because people feel that life is meaningful, understandable and manageable.'

The study was published by the American Psychological Association in the *Journal of Abnormal Psychology*.

Co-author Dr Michelle Newman, said: "Our findings suggest that people can improve their mental health by raising or maintaining high levels of tenacity, resilience and optimism.

'Aspiring toward personal and career goals can make people feel like their lives have meaning. On the other hand, disengaging from striving toward those aims or having a cynical attitude can have high mental health costs.'

3 May 2019

Why anxiety is good for our memory

By Tom Bawden

> *'Anxiety can help people to remember things – although there is an optimal level of anxiety that is going to benefit your memory'.*
>
> *– Myra Fernandes*

It may make us chew our nails or keep us awake at night, but anxiety does at least have the benefit of helping us to remember things we might otherwise forget, a study finds.

Being a bit worried makes us more alert – and so more likely to register and remember the sights and events we encounter, according to Canadian researchers.

But it is more than that. There is something about the negative thinking that arises from anxiety that helps to etch memories into our minds more deeply than if we regard something in a more neutral manner, they found – although it is unclear why.

'Anxiety can help people to remember things – although there is an optimal level of anxiety that is going to benefit your memory,' said Professor Myra Fernandes, of the University of Waterloo, Ontario.

'People with high anxiety need to be careful. High levels of anxiety can cause people to reach a tipping point, which impacts their memory and performance,' she added.

Stress tinges our interactions

It seems people are best at remembering 'neutral' events or information, such as a scene involving a lake or trees, when they are a little stressed but not so anxious that they are completely overwhelmed or suffering from depression, which can interfere with the functioning of their minds, said the researchers.

People who are a little but not too stressed tend to react negatively to neutral situations, so the memory becomes tinged by that more powerful, negative, emotion.

Take coffee, for example

So, for example, if a person is having a bad day and goes to a café they are more likely to interpret a neutral question such as 'Would you like milk in your coffee?' as some kind of slight and therefore remember it better, said study co-author Christopher Lee, of the University of Waterloo.

2 March 2018

Anxiety counselling

When anxiety moves from momentary worries like 'did I lock the door?' to incessant checking, locking and relocking, or you find yourself flooded with never-ending racing thoughts that feel overwhelming… It might be time to check-in, and reach out for support.

We all know what it's like to worry from time to time. That flutter of butterflies in your tummy before a final exam, sweaty palms before delivering that big presentation you've been working on for weeks… These are anxious feelings we can all relate to.

But how do we know when anxiety gets out of hand? When does feeling anxious move towards being an anxiety disorder?

Anxiety disorders come in lots of different shapes and sizes - phobias, panic attacks, sleep disorders, social anxiety… But one thing they all have in common is that they all have the ability to interfere with the pleasures of everyday life

> *'When anxiety moves from momentary worries like "did I lock the door?" to incessant checking, locking and relocking, or you find yourself flooded with never-ending racing thoughts that feel overwhelming… It might be time to check-in, and reach out for support'.*

Remember, you're not alone.

If you're feeling anxious and overwhelmed, it's important to remember that you're not alone. Anxiety disorders are a lot more common than many of us think. In 2013, there were 8.2 million cases of anxiety in the UK, and 40% of disabilities reported worldwide are down to anxiety and/or depression (unfortunately, the two often go hand-in-hand).

Remember that just in acknowledging your anxiety you're taking a really important first step towards turning things around. Fortunately, there's lots of support out there to help you learn how to better manage your anxiety and take the necessary steps to break negative patterns and move forward.

Whilst anxiety disorders can present themselves in lots of different ways, there are some common signs to look out for that might indicate it's time to seek support. We've compiled a list of potential symptoms that can accompany an anxiety disorder to use as a guidance below:

Racing thoughts

It's normal to have worries, particularly if you've been under a lot of pressure or something stressful has happened like losing a job or breaking up with a partner… But when those worries feel like they're endless, and they start to plague you day-in-day-out over a long period of time, then it might be time to seek help. Generalised Anxiety Disorder (GAD) is a common anxiety disorder that involves persistent worries. Whilst a person suffering from GAD might worry about the same types of things we all do – work, family, relationships, health – these worries can start to get out of proportion, or become so constant that they become overbearing. GAD is diagnosed when you find yourself feeling anxious almost every day, and the intensity of your worrying doesn't feel like it lessens over a period of six months.

Fears that don't match up

Fear is part and parcel of life. However, when fear falls out of proportion to what's actually happening, or you begin to feel fearful about taking part in everyday activities, then it might indicate that there's something larger at play. One example of an anxiety disorder centred around fear is someone who suffers from a phobia. Phobias bring about a feeling of intense dread or anxiety that might appear out of proportion to an outsider. A person suffering from a phobia is sometimes conscious that their reaction is 'over the top' or irrational, but the intensity of the fear is so overwhelming that it still prevents them from carrying out a particular activity.

Difficulty sleeping

Whether it's racing thoughts or an inability to 'switch off', many anxiety disorders end up having an impact on the quality of our sleep. You might find it difficult to fall asleep at night, or perhaps you're sleeping lots but still find yourself waking up feeling tired and groggy.

Compulsive behaviour

It's human to have little quirks about how we like things. Maybe we like keeping our house especially clean and tidy, or we prefer our morning cup of tea with the milk in first… However, when these habits start to become obsessive or compulsive – as though we 'can't' do something without them – then this might point towards a type of anxiety disorder such as Obsessive Compulsive Disorder (OCD).

OCD can look different depending on the individual, but it's normally characterised by unwanted thoughts or ideas that cause someone to behave in an obsessive, and often repetitive way.

Panic attacks

Panic attacks can be a frightening experience, particularly if it's something that hasn't happened to you before. Panic attacks bring on a sudden onset of intense physical symptoms such as: difficulty catching your breath, a racing heartbeat, sweating, dizziness, chest pains… Whilst panic attacks can be triggered by a specific activity (taking public transport or crossing a bridge, for instance), many people find that their panic attacks come completely out of the blue which can make living with the uncertainty especially difficult.

Tension in the body

There's no denying that the mind and the body are inextricably linked. This means that many people suffering anxiety will also experience physical symptoms. These might be awkward aches and pains, jaw clenching, balling your fists, grinding your teeth… Whilst Irritable Bowel Syndrome (IBS) isn't necessarily directly caused by anxiety, our digestive system is particularly sensitive to stress. This means that the two often coincide. In fact, it's thought that over 50% of people who suffer from IBS also suffer from an anxiety disorder.

Feeling self-conscious

Nobody likes feeling as though all eyes are on them, but very often this is the case for people who suffer from Social Anxiety. It's normal to have days when we don't feel like socialising, but a person who suffers from social anxiety will feel an overwhelming fear about being in social situations. They might worry for days – or even weeks – before a particular gathering or event. And afterwards, they might find themselves running it over and over again in the their minds, analysing what they said and what people thought about them.

Living with an anxiety disorder can be scary, overwhelming – and at its very worse, completely debilitating. But amidst all the discomfort, it's sometimes helpful to remember that even distressing emotions and sensations hold a purpose. Anxiety is in fact, a survival tactic hard-wired into us from our ancestors. It was anxiety that saved them from that grizzly bear lurking in the shadows whilst they were out hunting for lunch. The more highly tuned our fight-or-flight response was, the better chance we had of surviving. Of course, the difference is today we don't experience threats in quite the same way as our caveman ancestors… However, anxiety's purpose is still there to protect us.

The problem isn't anxiety itself, but rather when we get 'stuck' in its cycle and the brain gets wired into looking for potential threats. But there is a way out, and there are lots of tools available that can help. Therapy is great for anxiety because it provides the space to unravel uncomfortable thoughts and feelings in confidence. For many, bringing these worries into an open space and recognising them for what they are can bring about a sense of relief in itself. A good therapist will teach you tools to help accept and catch these anxious patterns in their tracks so they don't govern you in the same way.

Natural remedies for anxiety

These gentle natural remedies will help you to relax and combat your anxiety.

By Rosie Conroy

If you suffer with anxiety, then you may not have considered that there are some natural ways to relieve the symptoms of anxiety. These simple, natural ideas could make a huge difference to the way you feel and reduce the risk of you reaching anxiety levels that can often cause anxiety attacks.

Natural cures for anxiety can be used to treat anxiety attacks or just more generic anxiety symptoms, they're easier on your body than prescription drugs and come with very few, if any, side effects. Not to mention, natural remedies are often less expensive than reaching for the medicine cabinet as well.

The NHS describes the symptoms of anxiousness as being things such as restlessness, a sense of dread, feeling constantly on edge, difficulty concentrating and irritability. Anxiety can also translate into physical symptoms if severe, like dizziness, tiredness, stomach ache, pins and needles or aching tension in muscles, among others.

Anxiety can be brought on by many different things. Perhaps you become anxious when you think about money issues, you have a phobia of small spaces or even find it hard to cope with your family's day-to-day demands.

One of the simplest ways to combat anxiety is to identify the triggers. Once you know the triggers it will become much easier to consciously help yourself become less anxious.

In extreme cases where anxiety is left ignored it can lead to severe anxiety and panic attacks. If you're worried that you may be suffering from either of these then we would recommend speaking to your doctor or have a look at Mind's website.

While the benefits of colouring have been widely promoted since adult colouring books became hugely popular two years ago, there is now scientific proof that colouring for just ten minutes a day can reduce symptoms of anxiety as well as depression.

Originally praised for being a calming relaxation tool, psychology researchers at the University of Otago in New Zealand have now proved that colouring books could actually be used as a method to help manage mental health.

The study tested 115 women aged 18 – 36, and the results showed that those who were assigned a week of colouring-in tasks rather than other mind games such as sudoku had lower anxiety and symptoms of depression afterwards.

Our findings bode well for the potential psychological benefits of colouring-in, Dr Tamlin Conner, one of the authors of the study, said.

'In this way, colouring-in could be considered an act of everyday little-c creativity, in much the same way as gardening or gourmet cooking.'

'With its low risk and accessibility, we feel comfortable adding colouring-in to the growing list of creative activities for improving mental health outcomes.'

Tim Jacob, Professor Emeritus at Cardiff University's School of Bioscience has spent his career looking at the psychophysiology of smell, and he says that the right fragrance can have a substantial impact on your mood and stress levels.

'Lavender contains a natural anaesthetic called linalool, which is why it has a reputation for being relaxing,' he told the *Daily Mail*. 'Citrus scents have anti-depressive effects and mint has been shown to enhance sports performance.'

So depending on whether you want to increase your energy, reduce stress or get happy in a hurry, sniffing natural herbs and fruits could be an easy way to give yourself a boost.

Some of the most effective natural cures for anxiety are the simplest ones. It might sound obvious, but don't forget to breathe. Use deep breathing whenever you become aware of feeling anxious, to help you fall asleep, or even to deal with food cravings.

YouTube channel Big Think's experts suggest breathing in for half as long as you breathe out when you feel anxious – so for instance, inhale for five seconds, and then breathe out for ten.

This breathing technique for anxiety triggers a switch in your body's nervous system from sympathetic nervous system state (which is a very 'flight or fight' state for your body to be in) to parasympathetic nervous system state, which is known as a 'rest and digest' state, making you feel calmer and more relaxed.

It's thought to be impossible to feel anxious while practising conscious breathing. There is a famous technique called the 4-7-8 which is easy to do and can be simply fitted into your existing daily routine, ideally twice a day. Simply start by exhaling (it's important to always start breathing patterns with a breath out to release your feeling of stress). Inhale then, for a count of four through your nose, hold your breath for seven counts and slowly exhale through your mouth for eight counts. This process should leave you feeling lighter and more relaxed – it's even good to practise with little ones to help them nod off before bed.

For hundreds of years chamomile has been used as a natural remedy for lots of common conditions, everything from soothing tummy aches to relaxing people and reducing anxiety, in those few tense moments.

Some elements of chamomile act in the same way as sedative drugs like Valium, binding to the brain receptors and relaxing your mind. You can buy whole dried chamomile flowers to brew in hot water as tea, or buy pre-made tea bags in the supermarket (find them in the same aisle as normal tea bags). Alternatively, if you don't enjoy the flavour, you can take chamomile supplements, available to buy from chemists and health food shops.

Even Peter Rabbit's mum gets her baby bunny back to bouncing health with a little cup of chamomile tea, and they do say mums know best.

We all know that fruit and veggies are good for us, but do not underestimate vegetables as a natural remedy for anxiety – eating your five-a-day can really affect your mental wellbeing as well as your physical self.

Studies have shown that food, as herbal anxiety relief, can help or hinder your anxiety levels or anxiety disorders.

Try to avoid over-stimulating foods like sweets, coffee or white carbohydrates, all of these will give your body a sharp blood-sugar spike and then an equally sharp low afterwards, when you will notice you will feel more tense.

Incorporating more vitamin B into your every day meals will help level out your mood. B vitamins are believed to combat anxiety by affecting the brain's production of neurotransmitters. Leafy greens contain folate and legumes like peas and beans have lots of lovely B-6 vitamins, perfect for keeping you feeling calm.

Getting essential fatty acids into your body is really important to get your brain functioning at its most productive and naturally treat anxiety, especially anxiety symptoms in women.

Various studies have shown the positive effects drawn from incorporating Omega 3 into your diet regularly, from improving memory to reducing the feelings of anxiety and stress.

Try eating oil-rich fish like salmon a couple of times a week, or mackerel, which is just as delicious, and half the price! Alternatively, regularly boost your Omega 3 intake with fish oils which can aid in minimising the symptoms of anxiety and are available in capsules from pharmacies.

Taking a little time out of your day seems difficult for lots of people, especially if your anxiety is fuelled by feeling overwhelmed with what you need to achieve during the day, but mindfulness is a great natural remedy for balancing feelings of anxiety.

At first you may find it hard to concentrate but persevere and you'll be surprised at how quickly you can turn a few spare moments into a little piece of pure calm with meditation.

To meditate, choose a quiet place where you won't be disturbed. Sit in a position comfortable for you; try lying down, standing, sitting or even walking. Once you've found your ideal posture try to focus on being deeply calm and your breathing pattern. Once you feel you have settled into your meditation it's then time to examine the four foundations of mindfulness.

These are, mindfulness of the body, mindfulness of physical feelings and sensations, mindfulness of mental states and mindfulness of the consciousness.

For mindfulness of the body: Focus on each body part separately, like your head, heart, stomach, while continuing to keep your breathing deep and steady.

For mindfulness of physical feelings and sensations: Concentrate on whether what you're feeling is nice or not and mentally let go of any physical discomfort you might be feeling to reduce tension.

For mindfulness of mental states: Whatever pops into your mind, try to focus on this, whether it's dreams, memories, ideas, etc. Notice what you're thinking about and if it changes quickly to something else. Keep your breathing steady and controlled, and simply give a greater consciousness to whatever seems to come into your mind during this period.

For mindfulness of the consciousness: Note if you're feeling anxious, peaceful, stressed, angry etc. If you are feeling negative energy then the skill is to concentrate on this and gradually change the state of consciousness to let go of these feelings.

It will of course take a little while to get the hang of meditation so do persevere past the first few times you try it. Even if you feel like you haven't achieved much just remember that even ten minutes spent in quiet is good for your overall wellbeing.

Lavender is a classic remedy to help with getting to sleep. But recent research, according to *Health* magazine, has shown that breathing in the scent of lavender also lowers your heart rate and blood pressure, putting you into a relaxed state, which could be helpful with anxiety treatment too.

You can get your lavender fix in lots of simple ways. Treat yourself to a good quality essential oil and dab a little on your wrists. If you notice yourself getting anxious, inhale the smell until you are feeling a little calmer. Other ways to benefit from this fragrant dried flower is to put a few drops of its essential oil in a diffuser or oil burner, keep a bowl of dried flowers by your bed or even use some fancy bed sheet spray on your pillows before you turn in for the night. Or, why not try the Lush Twilight body spray that fans of the brand described as calming and soothing? Infused with lavender oil, it's the perfect way to surround yourself with the scent of lavender day or night.

We're not talking training for a marathon, but gentle regular exercise can improve feelings of anxiousness, by allowing mindfulness, taking time out and focusing on your breathing.

The Anxiety and Depression Association of America suggests that regular exercise can actually be just as beneficial as medication, and the good news is that apparently a ten-minute walk could be just as good as a 45-minute work out. Phew!

Try starting with a ten-minute walk in the morning before the rest of your usual routine or taking half an hour at lunchtime for a jog around the nearest park, if possible. Exercise also increases energy levels so you'll be doing yourself more than one favour if you keep up the good work.

Blueberries, strawberries and raspberries all contain plenty of vitamin C. Various studies published in *Psychopharmacology* show vitamin C-rich foods may help to regulate cortisol, which is a stress hormone. Throw a handful of berries into your yogurt or onto your cereal each morning, or blitz with some apple or orange for a tasty smoothie.

Ever since the days of ancient Greece, lemon balm has been well regarded for its soothing effects on the body and recently there has been lots of research that suggests lemon balm is effective in treating stress-related conditions and anxiety disorder.

Lemon balm is really easy to grow yourself if you've got a little sunny windowsill, balcony or garden. If you haven't got green fingers then pick some up at the shops, dried or fresh, and make some tea for yourself next time you notice you are feeling anxious.

Simply cut and wash a few leaves if using fresh and bruise them slightly to release the lemon-scented oil, pop the leaves in a cup and cover with boiling water to brew. After a few minutes you should have a lovely fragrant and soothing tea.

There is something so relaxing about having a hot bubble bath, and not just for your physical wellbeing; anxiety charity Calm Clinic suggest that a bath can be incredibly beneficial in reducing anxiety symptoms as well.

Like many natural treatments for anxiety, this is not by any means a long-term cure for anxiety disorders but it is a short-term relief for when your anxiety is peaking on a particular day.

In those circumstances, having a bath is a great way to manage your anxiety. Besides who doesn't like a nice soak?

So run yourself a nice hot bath and add bubbles, essential oils or anything else you fancy and soak for as long as you like. Try to fit in a couple of baths a week to benefit the most and use other anxiety-reducing aids like lavender oil, magnesium

or baking soda. You could even try turning your bathroom into a mini spa!

Breakfast might seem like the last thing on your mind when you are having a particularly anxious period, but again and again research has suggested that skipping meals and essential nutrients is only making the anxiety worse. Skipping the most important meal of the day could really be affecting your mood and stopping you treating your anxiety.

Dr Ramsey from Health.com advises anxiety sufferers; 'Many people with anxiety disorders skip breakfast. I recommend that people eat things like eggs, which are a satiating and filling protein, and are nature's top source of choline. Low levels of choline are associated with increased anxiety.'

If you are always in a hurry in the morning why not make yourself something the night before? Like a peanut butter sandwich popped in the fridge, some home-made granola muffins or simply just grab a couple of pieces of fruit to eat on the go – anything could help to get you on a better start to the day.

Sadly, baking soda doesn't reduce anxiety when baked into a cake but it is thought that baking soda could reduce tension when consumed in water and is recommended to help anxiety.

You can mix the powder in water and swallow like a medicine, the calming properties are thought to be down to it being so alkaline for the body.

Alternatively, add a good handful to a warm bath and let your body soak up all the muscle-easing goodness.

As with many natural remedies for anxiety, research is slightly limited as to the exact benefits of magnesium but there have been successful studies run in France, according to Calm Clinic, that note magnesium has positive improvements on patients who were taking the supplement regularly.

Magnesium is know to release muscle tension and there is a big link between how the body feels and how the mind feels. So if you can find magnesium crystals, then add a handful of these into a warm bath, or you can pick up supplements in most chemists to take each day to try and provide some herbal anxiety relief.

9 November 2017

Key facts

- What is important is the recognition that anxiety is normal and exists due to a set of bodily functions that have existed in us from our cave-man days. (page 1)

- People often experience physical, psychological and behavioural symptoms when they feel anxious or stressed. (page 1)

- The most common behavioural symptom (the things we do when we are anxious) is avoidance. (page 2)

- Difficult experiences in childhood, adolescence or adulthood are a common trigger for anxiety problems. (page 2)

- Panic attacks usually come on very suddenly and reach their peak within ten minutes. The peak generally lasts for five to ten minutes, but it can take much longer for all the anxiety to subside. (page 4)

- The first recognizable social media sites were created in the mid-1990s, so most youngsters under the age of 20 will never have lived without social media. (page 6)

- One in five people in the UK suffer high levels of anxiety at any one time; one in nine people worldwide will experience an anxiety disorder in any one year. (page 6)

- Anxiety and stress account for over a third of all work-related ill health and costs over £100 billion in England each year in lost productivity and reduced quality of life. (page 7)

- Anxiety can kill – even sub-clinical levels of anxiety can increase the risk of mortality by 20%. (page 7)

- While average anxiety levels reached a three-year low in 2018, about 10.3 million people continued to report high anxiety scores. (page 10)

- In the United States, over 16 million people have had at least one episode of major depression in their lives. Also, again according to the National Institute of Mental Health, over 19% of adults in the U.S. have had an anxiety disorder in the past year. (page 12)

- According to Ofcom's 2017 figures, 94% of adults in the UK own a mobile phone; and over three-quarters of those are smartphones. (page 14)

- A UK study found that smartphone users unlock their phones on average 85 times a day; and use it for about five hours each day. (page 14)

- Just under half of young people who use social media similar amount agree that it makes them feel 'inadequate'. More than half (57%) think social media creates 'overwhelming pressure' to succeed. (page 16)

- The Prince's Trust creates an index based on happiness and confidence which stood at 73 in 2009. It is now at its lowest level yet at 69. (page 16)

- Four out of 10 young people said they felt more confident online than they do in person, but that rises to almost half among the youngest age group, 16– to–18-year-olds. (page 16)

- Women living in the most deprived areas are over 60% more likely to have anxiety as women living in richer areas. (page 17)

- Anxiety disorders affect an estimated 40 million people in the United States, according to the Anxiety and Depression Association of America. (page 18)

- According to one study in 2010, people with panic disorder and social anxiety disorder are especially sensitive to the anxiety-inducing effects of caffeine. (page 19)

- Recent estimates suggest that over 30% of teens have an anxiety disorder. (page 26)

- A study that the journal *Psychological Science* published in 2009 found that when we imagine doing something, our minds and bodies anticipate the imagined action as though it were a real action. (page 29)

- In England alone, mental illness accounts for annual expenditure on healthcare of £14 billion and a reduction in gross domestic product of £52 billion owing to people unable to work to their full capacity. (page 31)

- It's thought that over 50% of people who suffer from IBS also suffer from an anxiety disorder. (page 36)

Agoraphobia

Fear of public places.

Anxiety

Feeling nervous, worried or distressed, sometimes to a point where the person feels so overwhelmed that they find everyday life very difficult to handle.

Body dysmorphic disorder (BDD)

A mental health condition where a person is preoccupied with their appearance which they believe has mnay flaws. These perceived flaws are often unnoticeable in others.

Cognitive behavioural therapy (CBT)

A psychological treatment which assumes that behavioural and emotional reactions are learned over a long period. A cognitive therapist will seek to identify the source of emotional problems and develop techniques to overcome them.

Depression

Someone is said to be significantly depressed, or suffering from depression, when feelings of sadness or misery don't go away quickly and are so bad that they interfere with everyday life. Symptoms can also include low self-esteem and a lack of motivation. Depression can be triggered by a traumatic/difficult event (reactive depression), but not always (e.g. endogenous depression).

Fight or flight response

Also called the stress response, this refers to a physical reaction the body encounters when faced with something it perceives to be a threat. The nervous system is primed, preparing the body to either fight the threat or run away from it. In the past, this response would have helped human beings to survive threats such as predatory animals. While this no longer applies to our modern lifestyles, our bodies will still react with the fight-or-flight response to any perceived threat - an approaching deadline, for example - causing many of the negative symptoms of stress.

FOMO

Fear of missing out. Feeling of anxiety, often prompted by posts seen on social media, that something exciting is happening elsewhere.

Generalised anxiety disorder (GAD)

Someone with GAD has a lot of anxiety (feeling fearful, worried and tense) on most days, and not just in specific situations, and the condition persists long-term. Some of the physical symptoms of anxiety come and go. Someone with this high level of `background anxiety` may also have panic attacks and some phobias.

Mindfulness

Mind-body based training that uses meditation, breathing and yoga techniques to help you focus on your thoughts and feelings. Mindfulness helps you manage your thoughts and feelings better, instead of being overwhelmed by them.

Panic attack

A panic attack is a severe attack of anxiety and fear which occurs suddenly, often without warning, and for no apparent reason. Symptoms can include palpitations, sweating, trembling, nausea and hyperventilation. At least one in ten people have occasional panic attacks. They tend to occur most in young adults.

Phobia

A fear of a situation or thing that is not actually dangerous and which most people do not find troublesome. The nearer a phobic person gets to the situation or thing that makes them anxious, the more anxious they get, and so they tend to avoid it. Away from the thing or situation that makes them feel anxious, they feel fine.

Post-traumatic stress disorder (PTSD)

PTSD is a psychological reaction to a highly traumatic event. It has been known by different names at different times in history: during the First World War, for example, soldiers suffering from PTSD were said to have `shell shock`.

Social anxiety disorder

Fear of social situations.

SSRIs

Selective serotonin reuptake inhibitors. A medication widely-used to treat depression and anxiety.

Stress

Stress is the feeling of being under pressure. A little bit of pressure can be a good thing, helping to motivate you: however, too much pressure or prolonged pressure can lead to stress, which is unhealthy for the mind and body and can cause symptoms such as lack of sleep, loss of appetite and difficulty concentrating.

Work-life balance

The concept of achieving a healthy balance between your career/work commitments and your home-life (family, friends, socialising, leisure activities, etc.).

Assignments

Brainstorming

- In small groups, discuss what you know about stress and anxiety. Consider the following points:

  - What is anxiety?

  - What are some of the common triggers for anxiety?

  - What are the common physical and psychological symptoms experienced by someone suffering with an anxiety disorder?

  - What kind of things do people do to cope with anxiety?

Research

- Do some research about BDD (Body dysmorphic disorder) When did people first start recognising this as a condition? What do you think has been the biggest contributing factor to the rise in diagnoses of this condition? Write some notes and feedback to your class.

- Thinking about specific phobia disorders, (look at the examples given in the article on page 4) conduct a survey to find out which phobias are the most common among your classmates. Write a short paragraph summarising your findings and include a graph or a pie chart.

- 'Emetophobia' is the clinical term for a specific phobia of vomiting. Do some research with a partner to find out the the meaning of the following common phobias:

  - aerophobia

  - hemophobia

  - achluophobia

  - ophidiophobia

  - acrophobia

  - coulrophobia

  - glossophobia

  - hydrophobia

  - trypanophobia

Design

- Design a poster that will help people recognise the symptoms of anxiety.

- Design a website that will give parents information about anxiety in young people. Think about the kind of information they might need and give your site a name and logo.

- Create a booklet to help students who are anxious about exams. Provide information on how to cope with stress, including relaxation techniques, tips on nutrition, advice on how best to prepare for an exam and anything else you think your readers would find helpful – you could even include some stress-busting meal ideas or suggest a relaxation playlist! Keep the tone light and fun and include illustrations.

- Read the article on page 7– *Feel better now? The rise and rise of the anxiety economy*. In small groups, design your own stress toy or anxiety-relieving product and create a brand and marketing campaign to promote it.

Oral

- In pairs, role play one of the following situations:

  - An employee telling their line manager that they are suffering from work-related stress, and the line manager's response.

  - A student telling their friend that they are feeling lonely and anxious, and the friend's advice.

- In small groups, create a three–four minute presentation, aimed at your year group, that explores ways of dealing with stress and anxiety.

- Choose one of the illustrations in this book and, in pairs, discuss what you think the artist was trying to portray with their image.

- As a class, discuss the impact social media has on young people's mental health – consider both the positive and negative feelings it can evoke.

Reading/writing

- Imagine that you work for a company where several of your colleagues have recently taken time off due to stress. Write a letter to your line manager, suggesting some changes you think would help to combat stress. You should think carefully about how you could persuade your manager that these are worthwhile changes.

- Write an article that compares the ways in which men and women experience anxiety differently.

- Write a blog post from the perspective of a first year University student who is struggling with depression.

Acknowledgements

The publisher is grateful for permission to reproduce the material in this book. While every care has been taken to trace and acknowledge copyright, the publisher tenders its apology for any accidental infringement or where copyright has proved untraceable. The publisher would be pleased to come to a suitable arrangement in any such case with the rightful owner.

Images

All images courtesy of iStock except pages 3, 6, 13, 16, 24, 26, 27, 28, 37, 38, 39: Pixabay, 4 & 34: rawpixel.com and 5, 8, 17, 23, 25 ,29, 32, 33, 39: Unsplash

Illustrations

Don Hatcher: pages 15 & 31. Simon Kneebone: pages 19 & 36. Angelo Madrid: pages 1 & 21.

Additional acknowledgements

With thanks to the Independence team: Shelley Baldry, Danielle Lobban, Jackie Staines and Jan Sunderland.

Tracy Biram

Cambridge, May 2019